5-INGREDIENT

natural recipes

5-INGREDIENT
natural recipes

New York Times bestselling author **PHYLLIS GOOD**

Creator of the bestselling *Fix-It and Forget-It* series

WALNUT STREET BOOKS

LANCASTER,
PENNSYLVANIA

walnutstreetbooks.com

5-Ingredient Natural Recipes

© 2020 by Phyllis Good

Softcover: 9781947597389
PDF: 9781947597396
EPUB: 9781947597396
Kindle: 9781947597396

Library of Congress Control Number: 2020911367

Design by Cliff Snyder
Photography and styling by Michael Miville Visuals
Additional styling by Nancy Stamatopoulos

5-Ingredient Natural Recipes is published by
Walnut Street Books, Lancaster, Pennsylvania
info@walnutstreetbooks.com

Books published by Walnut Street Books are available for special premium and promotional uses and for customized editions. For further information, please email info@walnutstreetbooks.com

Contents

I like to encourage families to eat at home as often as possible. Because when they do, kids experience belonging, do better in school, are more settled emotionally, learn appropriate food-serving sizes, and figure out how to take a part in conversation—all while eating around the table.

So your life is full, but you want to cook?

We're all trying a lot.

We want to eat healthy.

We prefer natural food straight from the garden, orchard, and butcher shop. We look suspiciously at processed foods and read the labels before putting anything into our grocery carts.

The recipes in this book use only natural, honest, wholesome, basic ingredients. With full-on flavor. No canned soups, no processed meats, no cake mixes, no stabilizers. I recommend organic ingredients whenever possible.

Many of us are short on confidence in the kitchen. How do we know a dish will turn out well?

Five-ingredient recipes are super-convenient. No fancy techniques. No breath-holding moments when you wonder if you're up to the job. These easy-to-prepare recipes make it possible for you and yours to eat at home. Regularly.

Each of these recipes calls for only 5 ingredients. Here's how I calculate that:

1. Water doesn't count.

2. Salt and pepper count as one ingredient.

3. Optional ingredients don't count.

4. If a recipe is for a sauce, the base you serve it over doesn't count.

Most of us live over-full lives. Who has time to cook?

I know. Which is why I present nearly all of these 140+ recipes with 2 cooking methods. You choose the one that fits your day.

Slow cookers and electric pressure cookers are convenient, but in opposite ways:

- If you haven't thought about what to make until it's dinner-time, good chance you'll reach for your electric pressure cooker. It's a dream for last-minute cooking.

- If you have thought ahead, you may have put the ingredients for your dinner in your slow cooker in the morning when the house is still peacefully quiet. The food cooks for hours on its own, and when it's time to eat, you lift the lid and call everyone to the table.

And sometimes you just prefer the flavor of an oven-roasted dish, or one you've steamed on the stove top or in the microwave.

Whatever your schedule, nearly every one of these recipes lets you choose which cooking method best fits your day!

Welcome to *5-Ingredient Natural Recipes*. Where you'll cook with naturally flavorful ingredients. Enjoy easy prep because you're working with only 5. Made whichever way suits your schedule. So what are you waiting for?!

One more thing—I invited some friends who are really good home cooks to join me in offering 5-ingredient natural recipes that they make. And they did! You'll see their names at the top of the recipes they and their families and friends love. You're joining a community when you cook from this book!

Phyllis Good

Meet the icons indicating the cooking methods for each recipe:

Slow Cooker

Oven

Microwave

Electric Pressure Cooker

Broiler

No Cooking

Stove Top

Grill

Metric Equivalents

Cooking/Oven Temperatures

	Fahrenheit	Celsius	Gas Mark
Boil Water	212° F	100° C	
	325° F	160° C	3
	350° F	180° C	4
	375° F	190° C	5
Bake	400° F	200° C	6
	425° F	220° C	7
	450° F	230° C	8
Broil			Grill

Length

(To convert inches to centimeters, multiply inches by 2.5)

1 in				=		2.5 cm
12 in	=	1 ft		=		30 cm
36 in	=	3 ft	=	1 yd	=	90 cm
40 in				=		100 cm = 1 m

Liquid Ingredients by Volume

¼ tsp				=				1 ml
½ tsp				=				2 ml
1 tsp				=				5 ml
3 tsp	=	1 Tbsp	=	½ fl oz	=			15 ml
2 Tbsp	=	⅛ cup	=	1 fl oz	=			30 ml
4 Tbsp	=	¼ cup	=	2 fl oz	=			60 ml
5⅓ Tbsp	=	⅓ cup	=	3 fl oz	=			80 ml
8 Tbsp	=	½ cup	=	4 fl oz	=			120 ml
10⅔ Tbsp	=	⅔ cup	=	5 fl oz	=			160 ml
12 Tbsp	=	¾ cup	=	6 fl oz	=			180 ml
16 Tbsp	=	1 cup	=	8 fl oz	=			240 ml
1 pt	=	2 cups	=	16 fl oz	=			480 ml
1 qt	=	4 cups	=	32 fl oz	=			960 ml
				33 fl oz	=	1000 ml	=	1 l

Dry Ingredients by Weight

(To convert ounces to grams, multiply the number of ounces by 30)

1 oz	=	¹⁄₁₆ lb	=	30 g
4 oz	=	¼ lb	=	120 g
8 oz	=	½ lb	=	240 g
12 oz	=	¾ lb	=	360 g
16 oz	=	1 lb	=	480 g

Equivalents for Different Kinds of Ingredients

Standard Cup	Fine Powder (flour, ex)	Grain (rice, ex)	Granular (sugar, ex)	Liquid Solids (butter, ex)	Liquid (milk, ex)
1	140 g	150 g	190 g	200 g	240 ml
¾	105 g	113 g	143 g	150 g	180 ml
⅔	93 g	100 g	125 g	133 g	160 ml
½	70 g	75 g	95 g	100 g	120 ml
⅓	47 g	50 g	63 g	67 g	80 ml
¼	35 g	38 g	48 g	50 g	60 ml
⅛	18 g	19 g	24 g	25 g	30 ml

SOUPS, STEWS, & CHOWDERS

Sweet Tomato Rice Soup

5 servings   *Prep Time: 10 minutes*

- 4 cups organic beef broth
- ¾ cup uncooked long-grain white rice (brown rice gets mushy)

- 4–5 large tomatoes, chopped, *or* 3–4 cups organic diced canned tomatoes
- 4 teaspoons honey
- ½–¾ cup whipping cream

6-qt. Slow Cooker
Time: 4 hours

1. Pour the broth, rice, and tomatoes into the slow cooker.
2. Cover. Cook on Low 4 hours.
3. Just before serving, stir in the honey. Mix well and cook 5 minutes, or just til heated through.
4. Turn off the cooker. Stir in the whipping cream til well mixed.

OR a 6-qt. Electric Pressure Cooker
Time: 25 minutes to cook; quick-release pressure

1. Pour the broth, rice, and tomatoes into the cooker.
2. Pressure cook on High 25 minutes (valve closed; Keep Warm setting off).
3. Quick-release the pressure.
4. Add the honey, stirring til it melts.
5. Gently stir in the whipping cream.

Tomato-Bread Soup

4 servings   *Prep Time: 20 minutes*   *from Kim M.*

- 1½ cups cubed stale bread, *or* sliced bread, cubed
- 1½ cups MIY Onion-Garlic Base (see recipe on page 192)

- 7 cups peeled and chopped tomatoes, *or* 2 28-oz. cans organic diced tomatoes
- ⅓ cup chopped fresh basil
- 6 cups organic vegetable *or* chicken broth

Stove Top
Time: 35 – 40 minutes

1. Place bread cubes in a wide, dry saucepan. Toast over low to medium heat til golden, stirring now and then to prevent burning. (Or toast whole slices of bread in a toaster, then cube.) Set bread aside.
2. Add MIY Onion-Garlic Base to the saucepan.
3. Stir in tomatoes, basil, and bread cubes. Simmer over medium heat 15 minutes, stirring occasionally.
4. Add broth and bring to a boil. Simmer 15 minutes over low heat. Taste. Add salt if needed.
5. If you wish, drizzle individual servings with olive oil.

OR a 6-qt. Electric Pressure Cooker
Time: 12 minutes to cook; 30 minutes to release pressure

1. Put toasted bread cubes, MIY Base, tomatoes, basil, and broth in the pressure cooker.
2. Pressure cook on High 12 minutes (valve closed; Keep Warm setting off).
3. Release the pressure naturally. Then open the valve to release any remaining pressure.
4. Taste. Add salt and pepper if needed.
5. Continue with Step 5 above.

Caramelized Red Onion Soup

6 - 8 servings　　　　*Prep Time: 5 - 10 minutes*　　　　*from Barbara L.*

- 2½ pounds red onions, halved and sliced thin
- ⅓ cup avocado *or* olive,oil
- ½ teaspoon kosher salt

- 4 cups organic low-sodium veggie broth
- ⅓ cup red wine

6-qt. Electric Pressure Cooker
Time: 35 - 40 minutes to cook; 15 minutes to release pressure

1. Place the onions, oil, and salt into the cooker. Stir well.
2. Sauté on High 15 – 20 minutes, stirring occasionally. Continue until the onions are caramelized. Turn off the Sauté setting.
3. Stir in the broth and wine.
4. Pressure cook on High 20 minutes (valve closed; Keep Warm setting off).
5. Release the pressure naturally for 15 minutes. Then open the valve to release any remaining pressure.
6. Taste. Season more if needed.

OR a 6-qt. Slow Cooker
Time: 7 - 8 hours

1. Place the onions, oil, and salt in the slow cooker. Stir well.
2. Cover. Cook on High 6 hours.
3. Stir in the veggie broth and wine.
4. Cover and cook on High another 1 – 2 hours, until the onions are falling-apart tender.
5. Remove the lid during the last 15 – 30 minutes of cooking to reduce the liquid.
6. Taste. Season more if needed. Float croutons, crostini, and/or cheese on top if you want.

The house will smell incredible while this cooks. Our family loves this recipe!

Butternut Squash Soup

4 - 6 servings   *Prep Time: 30 minutes*   *from Barbara L.*

- 3 pounds butternut squash, cubed, fresh *or* frozen

- 3 apples, cored, unpeeled, and cubed

- 1 medium red or yellow onion, diced

- 4 cups organic veggie broth

- 1 cup water

- salt and pepper to taste

6-qt. Slow Cooker
Time: 6 hours

1. Put the squash, apples, and onion in the cooker.

2. Stir in veggie broth and water.

3. Cover. Cook on Low 6 hours.

4. Purée with an immersion blender til smooth.

5. Add salt and pepper to taste.

Variations:

Include these ingredients if you want:

- minced garlic cloves in Step **1**

- grated cinnamon and nutmeg to taste after puréeing

OR a 6-qt. Electric Pressure Cooker
Time: 12 minutes to cook; quick-release pressure

1. Place all ingredients except seasonings in the cooker.

2. Pressure cook on High 12 minutes (valve closed; Keep Warm setting off).

3. Quick-release the pressure.

4. Continue with Steps 4 and 5 above.

Tip:

The soup can also be a delicious, plant-based sauce for mac and cheese. Mix together cooked pasta, this sauce, and any veggies you want. (It's a great way to use leftovers.) Top it all with bread crumbs and bake it at 350° 30–45 minutes, or til heated through.

Spicy Carrot Soup

4 - 6 servings   **Prep Time: 15 minutes**   *from Kim M.*

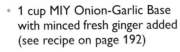

- 1 cup MIY Onion-Garlic Base with minced fresh ginger added (see recipe on page 192)

- 4 cup carrots, peeled and sliced

- 2 teaspoons ground spice of your choice—cumin, coriander, *or* curry are good options

- 4 cups organic chicken *or* vegetable broth

- cilantro to garnish

Stove Top
Cooking Time: 50 minutes

1. Sauté MIY Onion-Garlic Base and sliced carrots 5 minutes in a medium saucepan over medium heat, stirring occasionally.

2. Add ground spice and cook 1 minute.

3. Add broth and simmer 40 minutes, or til the carrots are tender.

4. Purée the soup with an immersion blender til smooth.

5. Garnish with chopped cilantro and serve.

OR a 6-qt. Electric Pressure Cooker
Time: 20 minutes to cook: quick-release pressure

1. Place the Base, carrots, ground spice, and broth in the cooker.

2. Pressure cook on High 20 minutes (valve closed; Keep Warm setting off).

3. Quick-release the pressure.

4. Pick up with Steps 4 and 5 above.

Tip:

We like this topped with MIY Seasoned Crumbs or Croutons (see MIY recipes on pages 210 and 214).

Black Bean Soup

9 - 12 servings   *Prep Time: 20 minutes*   *from Laura K.*

- 2 tablespoons olive oil
- 8 garlic cloves, chopped
- 3 – 4 1-pound cans organic black beans, drained and rinsed

- 4 cups organic chicken broth
- 3 cups water
- 1 batch Black Bean Soup Seasoning Mix (see recipe on page 216)

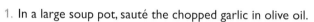

Stove Top
Cooking Time: 15 minutes

1. In a large soup pot, sauté the chopped garlic in olive oil.
2. Add the beans, broth, and 3 cups water.
3. Bring to a boil. Then cook, covered, over medium heat 10 minutes.
4. Purée with either an immersion or a stand blender. Fill a blender only half-full, remove the center cap on the lid, and hold the lid down with a heavy towel to keep the hot soup from shooting out. Repeat til you've puréed all the soup.
5. Stir in the Black Bean Soup Seasoning Mix (see recipe on page 216). Taste. Adjust seasoning if needed.

Optional ingredients for Step 1 before the garlic:

- 1 onion, chopped
- 2 carrots, chopped

- 2 celery ribs, chopped

OR a 6-qt. Electric Pressure Cooker
Time: 9 minutes; quick-release pressure

1. Sauté any of the optional ingredients, and then the chopped garlic, in oil in the cooker for 4 minutes, or til softened.
2. Stir in the beans, chicken broth, and water.
3. Pressure cook on High 5 minutes (valve closed; Keep Warm setting off).
4. Quick-release the pressure.
5. Follow Steps 4 and 5 above.

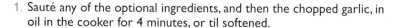

African Beef and Peanut Soup

6 servings   **Prep Time: 10 minutes**

- 1 pound chuck roast, cubed
- 2 cups stewed tomatoes, *or* 2 big fresh tomatoes, cut up, then mashed with your hands
- 1 tablespoon ginger root, chopped fine, *or* ½ teaspoon ground ginger

- ½–¾ teaspoon salt and cayenne pepper to taste
- 2 cups water
- ½ cup natural organic peanut butter

6-qt. Slow Cooker
Time: 5¼ – 6¼ hours

1. Stir together all ingredients except the peanut butter in the crock til well mixed.
2. Cover. Cook on Low 5–6 hours, or til the beef is tender but not dry.
3. Remove ¼ cup of liquid from the crock. Mix it in a small bowl with the peanut butter. Stir back into the cooker and cook another 15 minutes, or until hot through.
4. Serve over hot cooked rice, with lots of fresh toppings if you want.

Optional Ingredients:

1. Taste at the end of Step 3. Add additional seasonings, tasting after adding each one to make sure you aren't muddling the flavoring:

- 1½ teaspoons chili powder
- ½ teaspoon cumin
- ½ teaspoon smoked paprika

2. Make it a party and set out fresh toppings:

- grated coconut
- peanuts
- raisins
- chopped bananas
- apples
- oranges
- pineapples
- chopped bell peppers
- onions
- fresh tomatoes
- grated carrots

OR a 6-qt. Electric Pressure Cooker
Time: 55 minutes to cook; 30 minutes to reduce pressure

1. Sauté the beef on Medium in 1–2 tablespoons oil for a few minutes til well browned.

2. Turn off Sauté and stir in all remaining ingredients except the peanut butter.

3. Pressure cook on High 55 minutes (valve closed; Keep Warm setting off).

4. Release the pressure naturally, about 30 minutes.

5. Stir in the peanut butter. Close the lid to warm up the stew. Serve over rice and with all the fresh toppings you want (see Optional Ingredients 2 above).

Beef Barley Stew

8 - 10 servings   **Prep Time: 15 minutes**

- 3 – 4-pound chuck roast
- 2 cups chopped carrots
- 6 cups organic tomato juice, *divided*

- 2 cups uncooked pearl barley
- ¼ – ½ teaspoon salt and pepper, or to taste
- water if needed

 6-qt. Slow Cooker
Time: 8½ - 10½ hours

1. Put the roast, carrots, 4 cups juice, and barley in the crock.
2. Cover. Cook on Low 8 – 10 hours, or til the meat is fork-tender but not dry and the barley is soft but still chewy.
3. Lift the roast onto a platter and pull or cut it apart into ¾-inch chunks.
4. Stir the pieces of beef, remaining 2 cups tomato juice, and seasonings into the crock. Add water if you want a thinner stew.
5. Cook 30 minutes on High til hot through.

Optional Ingredient:

Add 2 cups green beans in Step 1.

 OR a 6-qt. Electric Pressure Cooker
Time: 55 minutes to cook; 40 minutes to reduce pressure

1. Sauté the roast at 300° for 5 minutes or so on each side til well browned. Lift the roast onto a platter.
2. Pour in 4 cups of juice. Stir loose all browned bits from the bottom of the crock into the juice.
3. Stir in the carrots, barley, and seasonings and return the meat to the cooker.
4. Pressure cook on High 45 minutes (valve closed; Keep Warm setting off).
5. Reduce the pressure naturally, about 40 minutes.
6. Cut the meat into bite-sized pieces. Stir it back into the Stew. If you want a thinner stew, stir in some boiling water.

Sausage-Lentil Stew

8 servings   *Prep Time: 15 - 20 minutes*

- 1 pound sausage, cut into ½-inch-thick slices
- 2 medium onions, chopped
- 2 cups organic tomato juice
- 2 cups lentils
- 1 tablespoon salt
- 2 quarts water

 6-qt. Electric Pressure Cooker
Time: 29 minutes to cook; quick-release pressure

1. Sauté the sausage in the crock for about 6 minutes, stirring now and then. When it's well browned, remove it.
2. Add the chopped onions to the drippings. Sauté 3 minutes, or until lightly browned. Turn off the Sauté function.
3. Pour in the tomato juice. Stir loose any browned bits from the bottom of the crock and into the onions and juice.
4. Stir in the lentils, salt, and water.
5. Pressure cook on High 20 minutes (valve closed; Keep Warm setting off).
6. Quick-release the pressure. Stir the soup and serve.

Optional Ingredient:

Add ½ teaspoon dried marjoram or thyme in Step 4.

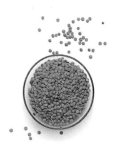

 OR a 6-qt. Slow Cooker
Time: 4 - 6 hours

1. Place all ingredients in the crock.
2. Cover. Cook on Low 4–6 hours, or until the lentils are tender but not mushy.

No-Beans Chili

8 - 10 servings   **Prep Time: 30 minutes**   *from Kristina S.*

- 1 large sweet Vidalia onion, diced
- 2 pounds lean ground beef
- 10 Roma tomatoes, peeled and chopped

- 4 sweet bell peppers (yellow, orange and/or red), seeded and diced
- ½ cup water
- ¼ cup MIY Chili Seasoning (see recipe on page 205)

6-qt. Slow Cooker
Time: 4 hours

1. In a large skillet—or in your slow cooker if it has a sauté function—sauté the onions and ground beef until the onions are translucent and the ground beef is no longer pink.

2. Place the onions, beef, tomatoes, peppers and water in the crock. Sprinkle Chili Seasoning on top and stir to combine.

3. Cook 4 hours on Low, or until the peppers and tomatoes are as soft as you like them.

Optional Ingredients:

Add 1 cup chopped celery or diced carrots in Step 1.

Tip:

Serve with rice and top with grated cheese, sour cream, and/or sliced avocado.

OR a 6-qt. Electric Pressure Cooker
Time: 10-12 minutes to cook; quick-release pressure

1. Sauté the onions, beef, and peppers in a bit of oil in the cooker for a few minutes til the vegs are softened and the beef is browned.

2. Add the tomatoes, water, and seasoning. Pressure cook on High 8 minutes (valve closed; Keep Warm setting off).

3. Quick-release the pressure.

This recipe is so full of fresh vegetables and flavor that you'll never miss the beans!

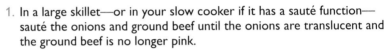

Mountain Soup Beans

4 servings   **Prep Time: 15 minutes**   *Soaking Time for dried beans:*
8 hours or overnight, or 2 minutes + 1 hour

- 2 cups, or about 1 pound, dry pinto beans
- 6 cups water
- 4–10 slices (your choice) thick-cut bacon, cut into squares

- ½ cup chopped onions
- ½ teaspoon salt and black pepper to taste

6-qt. Slow Cooker
Time: 5–12 hours

1. Soak beans in 6 cups water for 8 hours, or overnight, in the slow cooker crock. Or use the fast method—put the beans and water in a good-sized saucepan and boil for 2 minutes. Then reduce the heat and simmer for 1 hour.
2. Pour the beans and soaking water into the crock.
3. Stir in the cut-up bacon, chopped onions, salt, and pepper.
4. Cover. Cook on High 5–6 hours, or on Low 10–12 hours.
5. Taste and adjust seasonings.

OR a 6-qt. Electric Pressure Cooker
Time: 24 minutes to cook; 35 minutes to reduce pressure

1. Follow the soaking instructions in Step 1 above.
2. While the beans soak, sauté the bacon and onions in the cooker at 300° for 4 minutes or so.
3. Stir the prepared beans, water, and seasonings into the crock.
4. Pressure cook on High 20 minutes (valve closed; Keep Warm setting off).
5. Release the pressure naturally, about 35 minutes.
6. Taste and adjust seasonings. Stir and serve.

Split Pea and Ham Soup

6 - 8 servings   **Prep Time: 30 minutes**   **from Judith R-S.**

- 16 ounces, or 2 cups, dried green split peas

- 1 meaty ham bone, 2 ham hocks, *or* 2 cups cooked ham chunks

- 3 carrots, scrubbed and sliced

- 1 cup chopped onion

- 2 celery stalks plus leaves, chopped

- 1½ cups hot water

 6-qt. Slow Cooker
Time: 4 - 10 hours

1. Layer ingredients into the crock in the order given. (If using cooked ham chunks, add 30 minutes before the end of the cooking time.)

2. Cook on High 4–5 hours, or on Low 8–10 hours.

Optional ingredients:

- Salt and pepper to taste (some smoked or cooked pork may already have enough salt) and add a bay leaf in Step 1.

- Sprinkle fresh parsley over each individual bowl of soup just before serving.

 OR a 6-qt. Electric Pressure Cooker
Time: 1¼ hours to cook; quick-release pressure

1. If you're using a meaty ham bone or hocks, place them and 1½ cups water in the cooker.

2. Pressure cook on High 45 minutes (valve closed; Keep Warm setting off).

3. Quick-release the pressure. Stir in the dried split peas, carrots, onions, and celery.

4. Pressure cook on High 30 minutes (valve closed; Keep Warm setting off).

5. Quick-release the pressure. Lift out the ham bone. When it's cool enough to handle, cut the meat off and chop it.

6. Stir the meat back into the soup. Taste. If you wish, add seasonings.

Tip:

Add a dollop of plain yogurt to each individual bowl of soup just before serving.

VEGETABLE, PASTA, & GRAIN MAINS

Baked Macaroni & Cheese

4 - 6 servings   *Prep Time: 5 - 10 minutes*   *from Regina M.*

- 3 tablespoons butter
- 2½ cups uncooked macaroni, or another short pasta
- ½ teaspoon salt and ⅛ teaspoon pepper
- ½ pound sharp cheddar, or another favorite, shredded
- 1 quart (4 cups) milk

Oven
Baking Time: 60 minutes

1. Preheat the oven to 350°.
2. Put the butter in a 2-quart casserole and then into the oven to melt.
3. Pour the dry macaroni into the melted butter. Stir to coat.
4. Sprinkle salt, pepper, and shredded cheese over the macaroni. Toss lightly.
5. Pour milk over all. Do not stir.
6. Bake uncovered at 350° for 60 minutes.

OR a 6-qt. Electric Pressure Cooker
Time: 5 minutes to cook; quick-release pressure

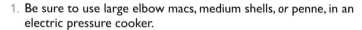

1. Be sure to use large elbow macs, medium shells, *or* penne, in an electric pressure cooker.
2. Melt the butter.
3. Mix all ingredients—except the cheese—together in the cooker.
4. Pressure cook on High 5 minutes (valve closed; Keep Warm setting off).
5. Quick-release the pressure.
6. Stir in the shredded cheese. Cover the cooker partially with the lid until the cheese melts and coats the macs. Let stand til the macs have absorbed all the liquid.

I don't like to mess up any more dishes than necessary, so this recipe is perfect. No pre-cooking the macs. This is also an-easy-to-succeed recipe for beginners and nervous cooks!

Asparagus Rotini with Fresh Mozzarella

6 servings   **Prep Time: 10 minutes**

- 1 pound uncooked rotini
- 3 tablespoons butter, *or* olive oil

- 3 cups fresh asparagus cut on the bias in 2″ pieces, *divided*
- salt and pepper to taste
- 4 – 6 ounces fresh mozzarella

 Stove Top
Time: 20 minutes

1. Cook the pasta according to package directions.

2. Before you drain it, scoop out 2 cups pasta water and set it aside. Then drain the pasta, keeping it warm.

3. Melt the butter in a stockpot. Stir in 2½ cups of asparagus.

4. Stir over medium heat just til the asparagus turns bright green. Mix in 1½ cups of the reserved pasta water, salt, and pepper.

5. Simmer over low-medium heat for about 5 minutes, stopping when the asparagus becomes crisp-tender.

6. Stir the cooked pasta into the asparagus and sauce. Toss.

7. Taste. Adjust the seasonings if needed.

8. To serve, pour the pasta and sauce into a big bowl. Top it with the remaining ½ cup raw asparagus. Break the mozzarella into chunks and scatter the pieces over all.

Variations:

1. Use any pasta that you prefer or have on hand.

2. Add ¼ teaspoon or more hot pepper flakes in Step 7.

3. Add 2 tablespoons chopped fresh chives in Step 8.

4. Purée the asparagus after Step 5 with an immersion blender til it's as creamy and smooth as you like.

OR a 6-qt. Electric Pressure Cooker
Time: 4 minutes to cook; quick-release pressure

1. Sauté the asparagus in the butter for about 2 minutes.

2. Then stir in the seasonings, uncooked rotini, and 6 cups water.

3. Pressure cook on High 2 minutes (valve closed; Keep Warm setting off).

4. Quick-release the pressure. If pasta water begins to shoot out of the valve opening, turn it shut. Wait half a minute, and then open the valve partially. If it continues, turn it shut again. Wait, and then open the valve just a bit. Continue until no more liquid sprays out, allowing the pressure to gradually release.

Mushrooms in Red Wine

4 servings   *Prep Time: 5 minutes*

Sauce:

- 1½ tablespoons olive oil
- ½ cup chopped onions
- 1½ cups red wine

- ¾ teaspoon salt and ¼ teaspoon black pepper
- ½ teaspoon dried thyme

- 1½ pounds small whole fresh mushrooms

- 1 pound short pasta, cooked according to package directions

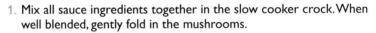

4-qt. Slow Cooker
Cooking Time: 4 – 6 hours

1. Mix all sauce ingredients together in the slow cooker crock. When well blended, gently fold in the mushrooms.

2. Cover. Cook on Low 3 – 5 hours.

3. Uncover. Cook on Low another hour to allow some of the liquid to evaporate and the sauce to thicken.

4. Serve over short pasta so you get both pasta and mushrooms in every bite.

Optional ingredients:

- Add 6 garlic cloves, minced, to Step 1.

OR a 6-qt. Electric Pressure Cooker
20 – 22 minutes to cook; quick-release pressure

1. Sauté the oil, onions, and mushrooms on Medium in the crock for 4 minutes.

2. Stir in the wine, salt, pepper, and thyme. Pressure Cook on High 10 minutes (valve closed; Keep Warm setting off).

3. Quick-release the pressure.

4. Sauté the sauce again on High—with the lid open—til the sauce simmers. Cook 5 – 7 minutes, stirring frequently, until the sauce thickens.

5. Follow Step 4 above.

Easy Oven Fajitas

6 servings   *Prep Time: 15 minutes*   *from Kim L.*

- 3 sweet bell peppers, sliced (1 red, 1 yellow, 1 green)
- 1 red onion, sliced
- MIY Fajita Seasoning

- 1 pound fresh mushrooms, sliced
- 4 fresh tomatoes, chopped
- 3–4 tablespoons oil
- 6–12 tortillas

Oven
Baking Time: 20 minutes

1. Preheat the oven to 425°. Grease 2 heavy sheet pans. Place the peppers, onion, mushrooms, tomatoes, and oil on the pans. Mix everything together lightly with your hands.
2. Roast 15–20 minutes, or until the vegetables are as soft as you like them. Drain off any juice that collects on the pans.
3. Mix the Fajita Seasoning into the roasted vegs.
4. Pile the mixture onto tortillas. Set out bowls of mashed avocado, sour cream, and cheese, for everyone to add as they wish.

Optional ingredients:

- 1 clove garlic, minced, added in Step 1
- shredded chicken from Lime Chicken Tacos (recipe on page 89) as a topping

 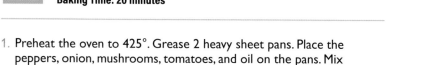

MIY Fajita Seasoning
Scant 2 tablespoons

- 2 teaspoons paprika
- 2 teaspoons cumin
- ½ teaspoon chili powder

- ½ teaspoon cinnamon
- salt to taste and ½ teaspoon cayenne pepper

1. Mix the seasonings together.
2. Use all of this mixture for 1 batch of Easy Oven Fajitas.
3. Store any remaining seasoning in a container with a tightly fitting lid.

Pasta with 5-Ingredient Tomato, Basil, and Pine Nut Sauce

4 servings **Prep Time: 15 minutes** *from Kim M.*

- 1½ pounds ripe tomatoes, cored and cut into ½-inch chunks

- 1 cup torn fresh basil leaves

- 2 teaspoons balsamic vinegar

- 12 ounces dry pasta

- 1 large garlic clove, pressed or grated

- salt and pepper to taste

- Pine Nut Sauce

 Stove Top
Cooking Time: 15 minutes

1. In a large bowl, combine the tomatoes, basil, vinegar, garlic, salt, and pepper. Toss thoroughly. Set aside to marinate while you cook the pasta. (You can prepare the tomatoes up to 3 hours in advance.)

2. Cook the pasta in a large pot of salted water according to package directions. Drain the pasta well and return it to the pot.

3. Add Pine Nut Sauce (recipe on page 202) and toss to coat the pasta.

4. Add the tomatoes and their dressing. Toss gently to combine.

 **OR a 6-qt. Electric Pressure Cooker**
2 minutes to cook; quick-release pressure

1. Short noodles—rotini, penne, farfalle, or shells—work better in the cooker than long noodles, which tangle and bunch up. Place the noodles in the cooker. Add 4½ cups water and ½ teaspoon salt.

2. Pressure cook on High 2 minutes (valve closed; Keep Warm setting off).

3. Quick-release the pressure.

4. Drain the noodles. Continue with Steps 1, 3, and 4 above.

Saag—puréed greens!

4 - 6 servings   ***Prep Time: 15 minutes***   *from Laura K.*

- 2 tablespoons oil
- 1 tablespoon, plus 1 teaspoon, Saag Seasoning Mix (see recipe on page 208)

- 1 pound fresh spinach, chopped
- 15-oz. can organic chickpeas, drained and rinsed
- 1 cup plain organic yogurt, regular *or* Greek

Stove Top
Cooking Time: 15 minutes

1. Heat oil. Add Saag Seasoning and sauté briefly.

2. Stir spinach into the pan, along with any water still clinging to its leaves. (If the spinach is dry, add 2 – 3 tablespoons water.) Heat just til the spinach wilts, 1 – 2 minutes. Let the spinach cool briefly.

3. Purée with an immersion blender. Or if you're using a stand blender, add only enough spinach to half-fill the blender. Cover, remove the central lid in the top, and cover with a thick towel before puréeing, holding it on tightly. Repeat til all spinach is puréed.

4. Place the spinach back in the saucepan. Stir in the chickpeas. Simmer 5 – 10 minutes.

5. Stir in the yogurt just before serving. Serve over or alongside rice.

Optional ingredients to add in Step 1:

- 1 onion, chopped
- 6 cloves garlic, minced

- 1 tablespoon minced ginger root

OR a Microwave
Time: 6 - 7 minutes

1. Place spinach in a microwave-safe bowl. Cover. Mic on High 4 – 5 minutes.

2. Follow Step 3 above.

3. Put the pureed spinach and chickpeas in the bowl. Cover. Mic on High 1 – 2 minutes.

4. Follow Step 5 above.

Dal – that warm Indian stew!

5 - 6 servings   ***Prep Time: 15 minutes***   *from Laura K.*

- ¼ stick (2 tablespoons) butter
- 3 cloves garlic, chopped
- 2 tablespoons + ¼ teaspoon Dal Seasoning Mix (see recipe on page 209)

- 1 cup red lentils
- 3 cups water
- 13½-ounce can organic coconut milk

Stove Top
Cooking Time: 30 minutes

1. Heat butter in a saucepan. Sauté garlic till soft. Stir in Dal Seasoning. Cook another minute.

2. Stir in lentils, water, and coconut milk. Bring to a boil.

3. Turn to low and simmer 30 minutes.

4. Purée using your immersion blender. Or use a stand blender, but do it in batches, making the blender a little less than half-full each time. Cover the blender, remove the center part of the lid, and hold a thick towel over the lid. Repeat til all the Dal is pureed.

5. Taste for seasoning. Stir in freshly squeezed lemon juice if you wish. Serve over or alongside rice.

Optional ingredients:

- In Step 2, 1 onion, chopped, 1 – 2 potatoes, chopped, 3 carrots, chopped

- 2 teaspoons lemon juice, Step 5
- toasted cashews, to top Dal and rice

OR a 6-qt. Electric Pressure Cooker
Time: 12 minutes to cook; 25 minutes to reduce pressure

1. Place all ingredients into the crock.

2. Pressure cook on High 12 minutes (valve closed; KeepWarm setting off).

3. Reduce pressure naturally, about 25 minutes. Pick up with Steps 4 – 5 above.

All On a Sweet Potato!

4 servings   ***Prep Time: 10 - 15 minutes***

- 4 good-sized sweet potatoes
- 2 cups small, fresh *or* frozen, Brussels sprouts (thawed)
- 2 tablespoons olive oil

- ½ cup dried cranberries, *or* dried cherries
- ½ cup crumbled feta, *or* bleu cheese

Oven
Baking Time: 45 - 50 minutes

1. Preheat the oven to 425°. Jag each sweet potato all over with a fork 4 – 6 times. Rub with butter or oil. Place on one-half of a greased sheet pan. Roast 25 minutes.

2. Toss the sprouts with olive oil. (If you have big ones, cut them in half first.) Spread the sprouts on the other half of the sheet pan.

3. Continue roasting 20 – 25 minutes, or until the potatoes and sprouts are both tender and even a little charred.

4. Take the sheet pan from the oven. Drop the temperature to 375°.

5. Cut through the length of each roasted potato, but not the whole way to the bottom. Push gently on the two ends of each potato so it spreads open. Spoon on the sprouts, dried cranberries, and cheese.

6. Put the filled potatoes back on the pan and into the oven. Heat 15 – 20 minutes, or til hot through.

Optional ingredients:

- Salt and pepper the sprouts before roasting them—and the baked, squeezed-open sweets.

- Add ½ cup chopped nuts to the toppings on the potatoes—pecans, walnuts, cashews all work well. Toast them first if you like.

OR a 6-qt. Electric Pressure Cooker

**Time: 20 minutes to cook; 20 minutes to reduce pressure;
13 - 15 minutes to microwave the sprouts and finished dish**

1. Pour 1½ cups water into the crock. Place the steamer rack on the floor of the crock. Lay the scrubbed and jagged potatoes on the rack.

2. Pressure cook on High 20 minutes (valve closed; Keep Warm off).

3. Reduce the pressure naturally, about 20 minutes.

4. Place the Brussels sprouts in a long, shallow, microwave-safe dish. Add ¼ cup water. Cover. Mic on High 10 – 12 minutes til tender, stirring every 3 minutes.

5. Continue with Step 5 above. Put the filled potatoes in the microwave-safe dish and mic 3 minutes on Power 8.

Lentils with Wine-Glazed Vegetables

6 servings   *Prep Time: 30 minutes*   *from Kristin O.*

- 3½ cups Italian Sofritto (recipe on page 190)
- 2 tablespoons organic tomato paste
- 3 cups brown lentils

- 6 cups water
- 1⅓ cups red wine
- 4 teaspoons organic Dijon mustard

5-qt. Slow Cooker
Cooking Time: 4 – 6 hours

1. Mix all ingredients together in the slow cooker crock.

2. Cover. Cook on Low 6 hours, or on High 4 hours, until the lentils and vegetables are tender and the sauce is syrupy. Cook without the lid for awhile if the sauce is too thin.

3. Serve with these toppings if you wish: chopped tarragon, microgreens or arugula, crumbled goat cheese.

Optional ingredients:

- 2 bay leaves added in Step 1
- 2 teaspoons salt, half added in Step 1 and half added in Step 3 if needed

- half a stick (4 tablespoons butter) and black pepper to taste, added when the dish is done cooking

OR a 6-qt. Electric Pressure Cooker
12 minutes to cook; 25 minutes to reduce pressure

1. If the vegs in the Italian Sofritto are uncooked, sauté them 5 minutes or so.

2. Stir in the remaining ingredients. Pressure cook on High 12 minutes (valve closed; Keep Warm setting off).

3. Release the pressure naturally, about 25 minutes.

4. Follow Step 3 above if you wish.

Baked Wild Rice & Lentil Pilaf

6 servings   *Prep Time: 10 minutes*   *from Kristin O.*

- ½ cup brown rice
- ½ cup wild rice
- ½ cup brown lentils

- 1 scant tablespoon organic vegetable bouillon, *or* 1 cube
- 1 tablespoon butter
- 2½ cups boiling water

Oven
Baking Time: 1 hour

1. Preheat the oven to 375°. Mound all ingredients but water in an 8″ greased baking dish with a lid.
2. Pour boiling water over all. Then stir.
3. Cover with an oven-proof lid or foil. Bake on the middle rack for 1 hour.
4. Fluff with a fork and serve.

Optional ingredients to add in Step 1:

- ½ tablespoon dried parsley
- 2 tablespoons chopped onions

OR a 6-qt. Electric Pressure Cooker
30 minutes to cook; 20 minutes to reduce pressure

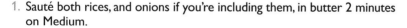

1. Sauté both rices, and onions if you're including them, in butter 2 minutes on Medium.
2. Stir in the lentils, bouillon, and water. Pressure cook on High 28 minutes (valve closed; Keep Warm setting off).
3. Reduce the pressure naturally, about 20 minutes.
4. Follow Step 4 above.

Tips:

1. Make this the base for bowl food. Add toppings—toasted nuts, sauces, greens, dried fruit, roasted vegetables, eggs done any way, and more.
2. The pilaf refrigerates well and is highly versatile. Most weekends, I double the portions and bake it in a larger baking dish, for easy meal options during the week.

Middle East Lentil Burgers

4 - 6 servings   **Prep Time:**   **Chilling Time:**   *from Margaret H.*
                    30 minutes   *2 - 12 hours*

- 2 cups cooked, cooled lentils
- 1 egg
- ⅓–½ cup plain bread crumbs, *divided*

- ¼ cup minced onion
- 1 rounded tablespoon Middle East Spice Blend (see page 206 for recipe)

Stove Top
Cooking Time: 4 - 6 minutes

1. Mix all ingredients together, using only ⅓ cup bread crumbs at first. See if you can mold a patty with that. Add the rest of the bread crumbs (up to ½ cup total) if needed.
2. Refrigerate 12 hours in a tightly covered container.
3. Heat 1–2 tablespoons oil in a large skillet. Drop ¼-cup amounts of lentil mixture into the hot oiled pan and gently push them into burger shapes.
4. Fry 2–3 minutes per side, or until browned and hot through.
5. Serve hot on buns with lettuce and sliced tomato, or over rice with shredded cucumbers and Tzatziki Sauce (recipe on page 199).

Variation:

Instead of the Middle East Spice Blend, use other herbs and seasonings that you like.

OR an Oven
Baking Time: 4 - 10 minutes

1. Follow Steps 1 and 2 above.
2. Pre-heat the oven to 375°. Grease a sheet pan well. Lay the burgers on the pan.
3. Bake 5 minutes on each side, or until browned well and heated through.
4. Or set the oven to broil. Position your oven rack—and the sheet pan of burgers—6 inches below the broiler flame.
5. Broil 2–4 minutes per side, or until browned well and heated through.
6. Proceed with Step 5 above.

Sweetly Flavorful Red Lentil Curry

4 servings   *Prep Time: 10 - 15 minutes*   *from June G-D.*

- 1 cup red lentils
- 6 carrots, coarsely chopped
- 1 onion, finely chopped

- ¼ cup golden raisins *or* craisins, *or* chopped dried apricots or figs
- 1 tablespoon curry powder
- 2 – 3 cups water

Stove Top
Cooking Time: 30 minutes

1. Pour all the ingredients into a sauce pan. Start with 2 cups of water. Stir together well.

2. Cover. Cook over high heat til the mixture begins to boil. Then turn it down to a simmer.

3. While you make a salad or rice to go along with the curry, stir it occasionally. If it's about to cook dry, add water as needed. The curry is done when the carrots are soft.

4. Serve over cooked rice.

Optional ingredients:

- 1 teaspoon salt, added in Step **1**
- ½ teaspoon fennel seeds, added in Step **1**

OR a 6-qt. Electric Pressure Cooker
Time: 20 minutes to cook; quick-release pressure

1. Pour all ingredients into the cooker. Use 3 cups of water.

2. Pressure cook on High 20 minutes (valve closed; Keep Warm setting off).

3. Quick-release the pressure.

4. Stir the curry, and serve over cooked rice.

Chickpea Curry

8 servings *Prep Time: 5 minutes* *from Kim L.*

- 1 medium onion, diced
- 2 14-ounce cans organic chickpeas, drained and rinsed
- 13½-ounce can organic coconut milk

- 1–2 tablespoons curry powder
- 1 teaspoon powdered ginger

Stove Top
Cooking Time: 30 minutes

1. Sauté the onions in a nonstick pan until translucent.

2. Stir in the remaining ingredients.

3. Bring to a boil, then turn down the heat to medium-low. Simmer uncovered 20–30 minutes, until the sauce thickens. Stir now and then to make sure the curry doesn't stick or scorch.

4. Serve over or alongside rice.

Optional Ingredients:

- 1 tablespoon oil and 3 garlic cloves, minced, added in Step 1
- 2 tablespoons flour, added in Step 2
- red pepper flakes and salt, added to taste, in Step 2

- 2 diced fresh tomatoes (or a 1-pound can chopped), added in Step 2
- Granny Smith apple, chopped, added right before simmering

OR a 4-qt. Slow Cooker
Cooking Time: 3–5 hours

1. Skip the sautéing and mix all ingredients (including any of the optional ones, except the tomatoes and apple) into your 4-quart slow cooker.

2. Cover. Cook on Low 3–4 hours, or on High 2 hours.

3. If you wish, stir in the tomatoes and apple. Continue cooking on Low one more hour, or on High one more hour.

4. Taste. Add seasonings if needed.

Black Bean Burgers

6 servings　　　　*Prep Time: 10 minutes*　　　　*from Kim L.*

- 2 cups homecooked black beans, *or* 15-ounce can organic, drained
- half a green bell pepper finely chopped, *or* 4-ounce can organic chopped green chilies, undrained

- 1 cup plain dry bread crumbs
- 1 teaspoon chili powder
- 1 large egg, beaten

 ### Stove Top
Cooking Time: 6 - 10 minutes

1. Place beans in a food processor and process until slightly mashed (you still should be able to see some whole beans). Remove from processor.
2. Mix beans, minced peppers or chilies, bread crumbs, chili powder, and egg.
3. Shape into 6 patties, ½-inch thick. Coat with cornmeal if you wish.
4. Cook in a non-stick skillet over medium heat for about 5 minutes on each side. Or preheat your grill pan over medium-high heat. Then lower the heat a bit and cook over medium heat for 3 – 5 minutes per side, or until crusty on the outside and hot in the middle.
5. Serve on buns with Sriracha Mayo (recipe on page 200), lettuce, tomatoes, and cheese.

 ### OR an Oven
Baking Time: 10 - 20 minutes

1. Preheat the oven to 375°. Cover a sheet pan with parchment.
2. Bake burgers for 5 – 10 minutes on each side, until the outside is starting to char and the interior is heated through.

Good Go-Alongs with this recipe:

Sweet Potato Fries with Caramelized Kimchi (recipe on page 131)

SALADS & SALAD DRESSINGS

Make It Blue! Salad

5 - 6 servings   ***Prep Time: 15 - 20 minutes, including the Dressing***

- ¾ pound fresh leafy greens—
  your choice of spinach,
  Romaine, spring mix…

- 2 cups fresh blueberries

- 4 – 6 ounces bleu *or* feta
  cheese, crumbled

- ½ – ¾ cup broken walnuts,
  toasted, if you have the time

- Honey Mustard Vinaigrette
  (recipe on page 68)

 No Cooking

Toss everything together just before serving.

Pears, Pecans, and Leafy Greens

4 - 5 servings　　　　　　　***Prep Time: 15 - 20 minutes, including the Dressing***

- ½ pound mixed fresh greens
- 1 – 2 good-sized pears, peeled or not, sliced
- ½ – ¾ cup broken feta, *or* shaved Pecorino Romano

- ⅓ cup broken pecans
- Honey Mustard Vinaigrette (recipe on page 68)

 No Cooking

Toss everything together just before serving.

Panzanella Salad

6 - 8 servings

Prep Time: 15 minutes, including the Dressing

Marinating Time: 30 minutes - 4 hours

- 4 cups chunked fresh tomatoes, as many seeds removed as you can

- 4 cups cut-up, day-old, crusty bread, pieces about the same size as the chunked tomatoes

- 1 cucumber, peeled or not, seeds removed, chunked

- half a red onion, chopped

- 1 bunch fresh basil leaves, torn

Dressing:

- ¼ cup olive oil

- 2 tablespoons red wine vinegar

- kosher salt and coarsely ground black pepper to taste

 No Cooking

1. Mix Dressing ingredients together in a jar with a tight-fitting lid. Shake until fully blended.

2. Combine all ingredients gently in a large bowl, including the Dressing.

3. Cover. Let stand at room temperature 30 minutes to 4 hours.

4. Serve at room temp.

Optional Salad ingredients:

- Add ¾ cup pitted black olives in Step 2

- Add ¼–½ pound fresh mozzarella cheese, torn into chunks in Step 2

Esther's Summer Salad

5 - 6 servings   **Prep Time: 15 minutes**   *from Susie S-W.*

- 1 large orange *or* red bell pepper, seeded and chopped
- 1½–2 cups fresh blueberries
- 2 cups bite-sized pieces of fresh pineapple

- 1 cup chopped English *or* Persian cucumber (the seedless kind with tender skin)
- ½–¾ cup freshly-squeezed lime juice

 No Cooking

1. Mix the first 4 ingredients together in a good-sized bowl.
2. Just before serving, pour in the lime juice.
3. Toss and serve in a glass bowl if you have one.

Optional ingredient:

- If you and the people at your table enjoy cilantro, chop and add some to the salad just before serving.

My friend Esther served this fresh,
delicious, and beautiful salad on a very hot
summer evening. We ate it with burgers
from the grill topped with slices of sweet
onions and just-picked local tomatoes.
What a wonderful summer-time meal!

Apple, Broccoli, & Craisins Salad

5 servings　　　　　　　　**Prep Time: 20 minutes**

- 2 crisp tart apples
- 3–4 cups fresh broccoli florets
- ⅓ cup craisins

- ¼ cup chopped walnuts
- 1–2 tablespoons chopped red onions

Dressing:

- ½–¾ cup organic vanilla yogurt

No Cooking

1. For added crunch, nutrition, and color, keep the peels on the apples. Include one with red skin and one with green. Chop into bite-sized pieces and place in a good-sized mixing bowl.

2. Stir in the broccoli, craisins, walnuts, and onions.

3. Gently fold in the yogurt. Serve immediately.

Cole Slaw

6 - 8 servings   *Prep Time: 20 - 30 minutes*

- half a good-sized firm head of cabbage, finely shredded
- half a small onion, grated or finely chopped

- ½ cup organic mayonnaise
- 1 – 2 tablespoons sugar
- 1 – 2 tablespoons apple cider vinegar

 No Cooking

1. Mix together the shredded cabbage and onion.

2. In a separate bowl, mix the mayonnaise til light and creamy. Fold in the sugar and vinegar.

3. Pour over the vegs and mix well.

Variation:

For added crunch and color, add 1 medium-sized carrot, grated, to Step 1.

Tip:

You can shred the cabbage in your blender or food processor. Chop it into slices, put a manageable portion into the appliance, cover it with water, and grate. Then drain thoroughly in a fine-holed colander before mixing with the other ingredients.

Wheat Berries with Feta and Plums

6 servings

Prep Time for salad and dressing: 20 minutes

Cooling Time for wheat berries: 1 hour

To cook the Wheat Berries:

- 1 cup raw wheat berries
- 1 quart water
- 1 tablespoon vegetable oil

 6-qt. Electric Pressure Cooker
Cooking time: 40 minutes; release pressure naturally, 30 minutes

1. Pour the ingredients into the crock. Pressure cook on High 40 minutes (valve closed; Keep Warm setting off).

2. Reduce pressure naturally, about 30 minutes.

3. Drain the wheat berries into a colander. Let cool to room temp.

 OR a Stove Top
Cooking time: 1–1½ hours

- 1 cup raw wheat berries
- 2–2½ cups water

1. Place the wheat berries and water in a saucepan. Bring to a boil.

2. Simmer, covered, 1–1½ hours. Check now and then to make sure the wheat berries aren't cooking dry. They're done when they've absorbed most or all of the water and are soft and chewy.

3. Set aside to cool.

To make the Salad:

- full portion of cooked wheat berries, chilled or at room temp
- 3–4 ripe fresh plums, sliced
- 2 scallions, sliced thin
- 2–4 ounces broken feta
- ½ cup chopped fresh mint

1. Place all ingredients in a large mixing bowl.

2. Pour in a full portion of Honey Mustard Vinaigrette (recipe on page 68). Fold together gently til well mixed.

Curly Pasta Salad
with Fresh Vegs

6 main-dish servings   *Prep & Cooking Time (going on simultaneously): 30 minutes*

- 1 pint cherry tomatoes
- 1 yellow bell pepper
- 1 cucumber

- 12 ounces uncooked rotini, as a base

- 2–3 cups fresh broccoli florets
- shredded Pecorino Romano cheese

- Herby Vinaigrette (recipe on page 67)

Stove Top
Cooking Time: 10-12 minutes

1. Start the water for cooking the rotini.

2. Meanwhile, cut the tomatoes in half, chop the pepper into squares, slice the cucumber, and cut up the broccoli. Put everything into a big mixing bowl as you finish with each veg.

3. Cook the pasta al dente, according to its package directions. Drain and cool it. Fold it into the bowl of vegs.

4. Make Herby Vinaigrette (recipe on page 67).

5. Add to the salad ingredients and fold together. Serve right away.

Optional ingredients:

Add these to the bowl in Step 2 if you wish:

- ½ cup chopped red onion
- 1 red bell pepper, cut into squares
- ⅓–½ cup sliced black olives

- 1 cup chopped zucchini, unpeeled
- 1 cup sliced fresh mushrooms

Festive Chicken Salad

4 main-dish servings   *Prep Time: 20 minutes, if the chicken is already cooked*

- 2 heads (alike or different) of your favorite lettuce, torn

- 1 big, *or* 2 medium, tomato(es), chopped

- 3 green onions, sliced on the diagonal

- Ranch Dressing (recipe on page 71)

- 1½ cups fresh *or* frozen (thawed) corn

- 1 pound cooked chicken, cut in bite-sized pieces

 No Cooking

1. Put the torn lettuce into a big mixing bowl.

2. Add the chopped tomatoes, sliced onions, corn, and chicken.

3. Add ½ cup Ranch Dressing (recipe on page 71). Fold everything together gently. Add more Dressing if you want.

Optional Ingredients for Step 2:

- chopped avocado

- 1 red bell pepper, seeded and chopped

- 1½ cups shredded carrots

- ¾ cup crumbled queso fresco *or* cotija, *or* shredded cheddar cheese

- half a seedless, minced jalapeño

- 1½ teaspoons chili powder, *or* ½ teaspoon hot pepper flakes.

Tip:

Make a Festive Chicken Salad Sandwich—stuff the dressed salad into pita bread or buns.

Chicken and Noodles Green Salad

4 main-dish servings   *Prep Time: 20 minutes, if the chicken is cooked and cubed*   *Chilling Time: 1 - 4 hours*

- 6 ounces uncooked rotini
- 3 – 4 cups cooked and cubed, *or* shredded, chicken
- full portion of Lemon Rosemary Dressing (recipe on page 70)
- ½ cup thinly sliced green onions
- 4 – 5 cups fresh spinach leaves, cut into ribbons

 Stove Top
Cooking Time: 10 - 12 minutes

1. Cook the rotini according to package directions. Drain well and cool to room temp.

2. Place the noodles, chicken, and a full portion of Lemon Rosemary Dressing in a large mixing bowl. Fold together. Cover. Chill 1 – 4 hours.

3. Just before serving, gently stir in sliced onions and fresh spinach.

Tip:

To cut the fresh spinach leaves into ribbons, pile up 4 – 6 leaves on a cutting board. Roll them up from the long side into a fairly tight roll. Then cut across the roll with a sharp knife with a sizable blade. They'll fall into ribbons on the board.

Spring Chicken Garden Salad

3 - 4 main-dish servings   *Prep Time: 30 - 40 minutes, if the chicken is already cooked*

- 1 pound fresh asparagus spears, *or* snow peas
- 2 tablespoons water
- 8 cups torn fresh spinach, *or* other salad greens

- 2 cups sliced fresh strawberries
- ¾ – 1 pound cooked chicken
- ¼ cup chopped pecans

- ⅓ – ½ cup Poppy Seed Dressing (recipe on page 74)

 Microwave
Cooking Time: 4 - 5 minutes

1. Break or cut off the woody bottoms of the asparagus spears. Cut the spears into 1″ pieces. Or cut off the pointy ends of the snow peas and pull off any strings along their sides.

2. Place the vegs in a microwave-safe dish, along with the water. Cover. Microwave on High 4 minutes, or til the vegs are bright green and crisp-tender.

3. Pour the vegs into a colander and run cold water over to stop the cooking. Drain.

4. Put the torn spinach into a good-sized mixing bowl, along with the sliced strawberries, cooked and cut-up chicken, and the drained vegs. Toss together carefully.

5. Just before serving, pour about half the dressing over top and fold it in gently. Add more dressing if you want.

6. Scatter pecans over top.

Cranberry Sauce from Scratch

1¾ cups   **Prep Time: 5 - 10 minutes**

- 12-ounce bag of fresh *or* frozen cranberries, *divided*
- ¼ cup white sugar and ¼ cup brown sugar
- ¼ cup orange juice
- 1 – 2 tablespoons orange zest
- ¼ teaspoon vanilla extract

 Stove Top
Cooking Time: 25 minutes

1. Scoop out about ½ cup of berries and set them aside til later.
2. Pour the rest of the berries into a saucepan. Stir in the sugars, orange juice, and zest.
3. Cover. Cook over low heat 10 minutes. Stir now and then til the sugars dissolve and the cranberries start to soften.
4. Turn the heat up to medium. Continue cooking another 12 minutes or so, til the cranberries begin popping.
5. Turn the heat back to low. Stir in the vanilla and the cranberries you've set aside. Heat just til they're warm but not popping.
6. Cool before serving.

 **OR a 6-qt. Electric Pressure Cooker**
Cooking Time: 3 - 4 minutes to cook; 20 - 30 minutes to release pressure

1. Put all ingredients except the vanilla into the cooker. Stir til well mixed.
2. Pressure cook on High 3 minutes—or 4 if you double the ingredient amounts (valve closed; Keep Warm setting off). Release the pressure naturally, 20 – 30 minutes.
3. Stir in the vanilla. Mash the cranberries til the sauce is as smooth or as chunky as you like.
4. Cool before serving.

Tip: Double all the ingredient amounts for this to be a full side dish and not just a garnish.

Strawberry Spinach Salad with Ham

4 main-dish servings   *Prep Time: 25 - 30 minutes*

- 1 pound asparagus spears
- 2 tablespoons water
- ¾ pound cooked *or* baked ham

- 8–10 cups fresh spinach, torn, *or* cut into ribbons
- 2 cups sliced fresh strawberries
- ¼ cup sliced almonds

- ¼ cup Poppy Seed Dressing (recipe on page 74), mixed with 1 teaspoon orange zest and 1 tablespoon orange juice

Microwave
Cooking Time: 4 - 8 minutes

1. Cut any woody bottoms off the asparagus. Cut the remaining spears diagonally in 1" lengths.

2. Place in a microwave-safe dish, along with 2 tablespoons of water. Cover. Cook on High 2 minutes. Stir. Cover and mic again on High for 2 minutes, or until the asparagus is bright green and crisp-tender.

3. Plunge the asparagus into cold water. Drain well. Place in a big mixing bowl.

4. Stir in the ham.

5. Prepare the Poppy Seed Dressing. Set aside til ready to serve.

6. Then gently fold in the spinach, strawberries, and Dressing. Scatter almonds over top and serve.

Variations:

1. Use cooked or grilled turkey or chicken instead of ham.

2. Use fresh blueberries instead of fresh strawberries.

Freezer Cucumber Salad

8 - 10 servings **Prep Time: 10 minutes** *from Kim M.*

- 8 slender cucumbers, peeled or not
- 2 tablespoons salt

- ⅔ cup oil
- ⅔ cup apple cider vinegar
- ⅓ cup white sugar

No Cooking
Standing Time: 2 hours; Chilling Time: 4 - 8 hours

1. Slice the cucumbers into thin slices.

2. In a large bowl, mix the sliced cucumbers with salt.

3. Let stand 2 hours.

4. Drain the cucumbers and rinse with cold water. Drain well.

5. Add oil, vinegar, and sugar to the drained cucumbers and mix thoroughly.

6. Refrigerate several hours or overnight.

7. Pack cucumbers and pickling liquid in freezer containers, leaving 1 inch of head space. Cover and freeze.

8. Allow to thaw before serving.

Optional ingredient:

- thinly sliced onion, in Step 2

Have an abundance of cucumbers?!

Love cucumbers year-round?

Don't miss this easy solution.

Herby Vinaigrette

¾ cup   **Prep Time: 5 minutes**

- 6 tablespoons apple cider vinegar
- 6 tablespoons oil

- 1 teaspoon snipped fresh chives
- ½ teaspoon dried tarragon
- ½ teaspoon dried dill

 No Cooking

1. Pour all ingredients into a jar with a tight-fitting lid. Shake together til fully blended.

2. Pour over salad and mix together gently but well.

Optional ingredient:

- Add ½ teaspoon salt to Step 1.

Honey Mustard Vinaigrette

¾ cup   ***Prep Time: 5 minutes***

- 6 tablespoons oil
- 2 tablespoons organic brown mustard
- 2 tablespoons honey*

- 2 tablespoons fresh lemon juice
- ½ teaspoon salt

 No Cooking

1. Place everything in a jar with a tight-fitting lid. Shake together til fully blended.
2. Use immediately, or store covered in the fridge.

Variation:

Use apple cider or raspberry vinegar instead of lemon juice.

*Tip:

Warm the honey for 1–2 minutes in the microwave. That makes it more willing to mix with the other dressing ingredients.

Lemon Rosemary Dressing

Makes ¾ cup dressing   *Prep Time: 5 minutes*

- ½ cup olive oil
- ¼ cup fresh lemon juice
- 1½ teaspoons garlic salt

- 1 teaspoon dry mustard
- 1 teaspoon dry rosemary leaves

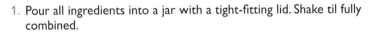

No Cooking

1. Pour all ingredients into a jar with a tight-fitting lid. Shake til fully combined.
2. Use immediately, or store covered in the fridge.

Optional ingredient:

- Add ½ teaspoon coarsely ground black pepper.

Ranch Dressing

scant 1 cup   **Prep Time: 5 - 7 minutes**

- ⅔ cup organic cottage cheese *or* ricotta
- 2 tablespoons milk
- 1 tablespoon tarragon vinegar

- 1 garlic clove, minced
- 1 tablespoon thinly sliced green onions

 No Cooking

1. Blend all the ingredients—except the sliced onions—in a blender til smooth.
2. Add the onion slices. Blend just til combined.
3. Use immediately, or store in the fridge in a jar with a tight-fitting lid.

Cilantro Dressing

1⅓ cups　　　　　**Prep Time: 10 minutes**　　　　*from Kim M.*

- ¾ cup fresh cilantro leaves and thin stems
- ½ cup organic plain Greek yogurt

- 2 cloves garlic
- ¼ cup apple cider vinegar, *or* white wine vinegar
- ¼ cup olive oil

 No Cooking

---

1. Place cilantro, Greek yogurt, and garlic in a somewhat tall, narrow container and pulse with an immersion blender until smooth. (Or use your food processor or blender.)
2. Add vinegar and blend in.
3. While blending, add olive oil in a slow stream until the dressing emulsifies.
4. Use immediately, or store in the fridge in a jar with a tight-fitting lid.

Optional ingredients:

- juice from one lime, added in Step 1
- salt to taste, added at the end

Tips:

1. If the dressing separates, shake to mix before serving.
2. Great dressing for a Tex-Mex salad with avocado, beans, and tortilla chips.

Poppy Seed Dressing

1 cup dressing   **Prep Time: 5 minutes**

- ½ cup oil
- ¼ cup honey
- ¼ cup apple cider vinegar

- ¼ teaspoon dry mustard
- 1½ teaspoons poppy seeds

 No Cooking

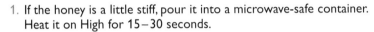

1. If the honey is a little stiff, pour it into a microwave-safe container. Heat it on High for 15–30 seconds.

2. Pour it and the other ingredients—except the poppy seeds—into a blender and blend for 2 minutes.

3. Stir in the poppy seeds.

4. Pour the dressing over the salad. Store any leftover dressing in a container with a tight-fitting lid. Refrigerate.

POULTRY

Creamy Stuffed Chicken Breasts Wrapped in Prosciutto

4 servings   **Prep Time: 20 - 30 minutes**   *from Carol and Robert M.*

- 4 thick boneless skinless chicken breasts
- 8 ounces fresh mozzarella cheese
- bunch of fresh basil, *or* sage leaves
- 6 ounces thinly sliced prosciutto, *or* bacon

Oven
Roasting Time: 25 - 30 minutes

1. Butterfly each breast: stand each one on its side and cut down through—but not the whole way—so you can open it like a book. Or pound each breast til it's ¼ – ½″ thick.
2. Preheat the oven to 375°. Grease a rimmed baking sheet.
3. Cut the cheese into thin slices. Lay it over the open breasts, keeping it about an inch away from the edges.
4. Cover the cheese with the herby leaves.
5. Holding the cheese and leaves in place, roll up each breast, short end to short end. Use 2 toothpicks to hold each breast roll closed.
6. Wrap long pieces of prosciutto around each breast, overlapping the pieces a bit.
7. Keep the toothpicks if needed, or discard if the rolls stay closed.
8. Lay the rolls on the prepared pan. Roast 25 – 30 minutes, depending on how big the breasts are. Or until an instant-read meat thermometer stuck into the thickest part of the breasts registers 160°.
9. Let stand 5 minutes before serving so the juices can gather themselves.

Tip:

You can easily multiply this recipe for many more servings in the oven and roast them for the same amount of time.

OR a 6-qt. Slow Cooker
Cooking Time: 3½ - 4½ hours

1. Use thick boneless skinless chicken thighs instead of breasts. They hold up much better when slow cooking.
2. Follow Steps 1 – 7. Lay the prepped thighs in a single layer into the crock. Or stagger them if you have to create a second layer.
3. Cover. Cook on Low 3½ – 4½ hours.

1. If you have to stack the stuffed thighs in a slow cooker crock, you may need to add another 30–60 minutes of cooking time. Begin checking after 4½ hours, and check every 30 minutes thereafter so you don't overcook the meat. The meat is done when an instant-read meat thermometer stuck into the thickest part of the thigh registers 160°. They will continue cooking after being removed from the heat.

2. The prosciutto or bacon will not brown, so you may want to lift the fully cooked thighs onto a baking sheet and run them under the broiler for a minute or so. Watch carefully so you brown but don't burn the meat.

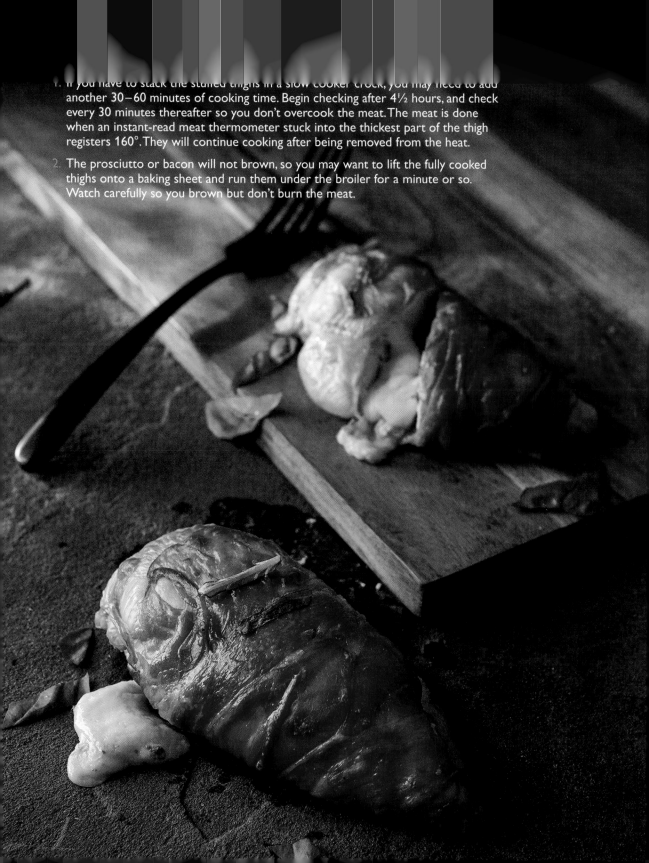

Roast Chicken—
with a future!

4 servings   *Prep Time: 7-10 minutes*

- olive oil
- salt and pepper
- 3½–4 pounds boneless, skinless chicken thighs

- whole medium onion
- whole lemon
- ¾ cup water

6-qt. Slow Cooker
Cooking Time: 3½ - 4½ hours

1. Rub the thighs all over with olive oil. Salt and pepper them top and bottom. Place in the cooker, staggering the layers.

2. Quarter the onion and lay over the thighs. Cut the lemon in half and squeeze its juice over top.

3. Pour water down along the interior wall of the cooker.

4. Cover. Cook on Low 3½–4½ hours, or til an instant-read meat thermometer inserted into the thickest parts of the thighs registers 160°.

5. When fully cooked, shred or chunk the meat. Box it up in 1- or 2-cup amounts and label the containers before freezing. Do the same with the broth.

6. Use the cooked chicken in bowls; sandwiches; pizzas; salads; over rice, potatoes, or pastas; in broth or gravy; in tacos or tortillas; in soups. Or in Chicken Roasht (recipe on page 87). Add seasonings and sauces to fit the dish. You've just made a big deposit on future meals!

OR a 6-qt. Electric Pressure Cooker
Cooking Time: 21 - 24 minutes; 1 hour to reduce pressure naturally

1. Pour 2 cups water into the crock. Put in the steamer rack. Follow Steps 1 and 2 above.

2. Pressure cook on High 21–24 minutes, about 6 minutes per pound (valve closed; Keep Warm setting off).

3. Reduce the pressure naturally; about an 1 hour.

4. Continue with Steps 5–6 above.

Whole Chicken with Vegs in a Pot

4 - 6 servings   *Prep Time: 20 - 30 minutes*   *from Judith R-S.*

- 3 medium potatoes, peeled or not, and sliced
- 3 medium carrots, sliced

- 1 large onion, sliced
- 3 – 4-pound whole chicken
- salt and pepper to taste

 6-qt. Slow Cooker
Cooking Time: 4 - 10 hours

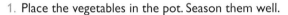

1. Place the vegetables in the pot. Season them well.

2. Season the chicken on all sides. Set it on top.

3. Cover. Cook on High 4 – 5 hours, or on Low 8 – 10 hours.

4. After 4 hours (on High) or 8 hours (on Low), wiggle the legs to see if the chicken is tender. Or insert an instant-read meat thermometer into the thick part of a thigh (but not against the bone). If it registers 160°, it's finished.

5. Carve the chicken. Serve it on a platter with the vegetables. Or debone the bird when it's cool enough to handle. Stir the meat through the vegs.

OR a 6-qt. Electric Pressure Cooker
Cooking Time: 36 minutes; 30 - 60 minutes to reduce pressure naturally

1. Pour 2 cups water or broth into the crock. Place a steamer rack in the cooker.

2. Follow Steps 1 and 2 above. Bird should have its breast side up.

3. Pressure Cook on High 36 minutes (valve closed; Keep Warm setting off).

4. Reduce the pressure naturally, about 30 – 60 minutes.

5. Use large tongs and a sturdy spatula or spoon to lift the chicken out of the pot. Be careful of the very hot juices that will run out of the bird when you lift it.

6. Follow Step 5 above.

Chicken Parm

6 servings   *Prep Time: 20 - 30 minutes*

- 1 cup freshly grated Parmesan cheese

- 2 cups fine bread, *or* panko, crumbs

- 5⅓ tablespoons (⅓ cup) butter, melted

- ⅓ cup organic *or* homemade pesto

- 6 boneless, skinless chicken breast halves

 Oven
Roasting Time: 20 - 35 minutes

1. Mix the grated cheese, bread crumbs, and butter together in a shallow dish, large enough to hold a chicken breast half.

2. Preheat the oven to 400°. Grease a 9″ × 13″ baking dish.

3. Dip the breasts one by one into the cheese-crumb mixture, coating them well on both sides.

4. Lay into the baking dish. Spread pesto on top of each breast.

5. Bake uncovered 20 – 35 minutes, depending on the breasts' thickness.

Variations:

1. When the chicken is finished, top each piece with a slice of fresh mozzarella cheese. Let it melt from the heat of the chicken, or slide it under the broiler for a few seconds, watching carefully.

2. Warm your favorite marinara sauce. Spoon part of it onto individual plates. Top with the finished chicken and another spoon of marinara sauce over each piece.

 OR a Broiler
Broiling Time: 6 - 9 minutes

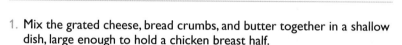

1. Follow Step 1 above. Preheat the broiler. Grease a sheet pan.

2. Follow Steps 3 – 4 above. Lay coated breasts on the sheet pan.

3. Broil 4 – 5 minutes on Side 1. Flip and broil 2 – 4 minutes on Side 2.

Chicken with Peanut Sauce

6 servings   **Prep Time: 10 - 15 minutes**

- 3 tablespoons oil, *divided*
- 3 pounds chicken thighs
- 1 large onion, sliced
- MIY Peanut Sauce

Stove Top
Cooking Time: 40 - 45 minutes

1. Heat 2 tablespoons oil over medium heat in a large skillet or saucepan.
2. Lay in the thighs, leaving space between them so they brown rather than steam in their own juices. Do two batches instead of crowding them.
3. Remove the well browned, nearly tender chicken from the pan. Keep it warm under foil.
4. Add the remaining oil to the skillet. Sauté the onion slices over medium-high heat until softened.
5. Prepare the Peanut Sauce below.
6. Return the chicken to the pan, settling it into the Sauce. Cover and cook over medium heat until tender.
7. Taste. Adjust seasoning if needed. Serve over hot cooked rice.

MIY Peanut Sauce
3 - 4 cups

- 1 cup chopped fresh, or organic canned, tomatoes
- ¼ cup organic tomato paste
- ½ cup natural, organic peanut butter
- ¾ – 1 cup water, depending on the sauciness you like
- 1 bay leaf

1. Stir the tomatoes, tomato paste, peanut butter, water, and bay leaf into the sautéed onions.
2. Cook over medium-high heat, stirring continually until the sauce is smooth.

Braised Chicken from the East

6 servings   **Prep Time: 7 minutes**

- 3–4 pounds boneless, skinless chicken thighs

- 3 tablespoons organic hot sweet mustard, *or 2 tablespoons organic hot mustard + 1 tablespoon honey*

- 2–3 tablespoons organic soy sauce

- 1 tablespoon finely minced fresh ginger root, *or 1 teaspoon ground ginger*

- 1 teaspoon ground cumin

6-qt. Slow-Cooker
Cooking Time: 3½ – 5½ hours

1. Stack the thighs into the crock, staggering them if you have to make more than one layer.

2. Combine the mustard, soy sauce, ginger, and cumin til well mixed.

3. Pour over the thighs, including those that may be partly covered by others.

4. Cover. Cook on Low 3½ to 4½ hours, or til an instant-read meat thermometer registers 160°. Or cook 5½ hours to shred the meat and mix it with the sauce.

5. Serve with, or over top of, your favorite rice or pasta.

Optional ingredients:

In Step 2, add chopped garlic, olive oil, sesame oil, organic teriyaki sauce, cardamom, dry vermouth, and/or organic oyster sauce.

OR a 6-qt. Electric Pressure Cooker
Cooking Time: 16 minutes; quick-release pressure

1. Follow Steps 1–3, using the electric pressure cooker crock. Consider the optional ingredients.

2. Pressure cook on High 16 minutes (valve closed; Keep Warm setting off). Quick-release the pressure.

3. Serve the chicken with the sauce spooned over top. Or shredded and mixed into the sauce. Follow Step 5 above.

Chicken and Black Beans

4 - 5 servings   *Prep Time: 10 minutes*   *from Meredith M.*

- 4 or 5 boneless skinless chicken thighs, 5 – 6 ounces each, seasoned
- 2 cups cooked black beans, well drained

- 2 cups fresh, frozen, *or* canned corn, drained
- 2 cups organic salsa, *or* Salsa-In-No-Time (recipe on page 176)
- 2 cups grated cheddar cheese

 6-qt. Slow Cooker
Cooking Time: 4½ - 5½ hours

1. Place the seasoned chicken in the crock.
2. Top with a layer of black beans, followed by a layer of corn. Spoon salsa over top.
3. Cook on High 4 – 5 hours, or til the chicken registers 160° on an instant-read meat thermometer.
4. Scatter grated cheese over top. Let stand, covered, 30 minutes.
5. Leave the thighs whole and serve over rice. Or shred the meat with two forks and stir into the sauce.

 **OR a 6-qt. Electric Pressure Cooker**
Cooking Time: 16 minutes; quick-release pressure

1. Place the seasoned chicken in the crock.
2. Follow Step 2 above.
3. Pressure cook on High 16 minutes (valve closed; Keep Warm setting off).
4. Quick-release the pressure.
5. Then continue with Steps 4 and 5 above.

Chicken, Rice and Rosemary Biryani

4 servings   ***Prep Time: 10 minutes***   *from Joanna R-McD.*

- 4 large bone-in, skin-on chicken thighs
- 2 onions, sliced
- 1½ cups uncooked basmati rice

- 3 teaspoons dried rosemary
- 3 cups water
- salt and pepper

Stove Top
Cooking Time: 55 - 60 minutes

1. On medium-high heat, brown the chicken in 2 batches in a large no-stick frying pan until its skin is crisp.
2. Remove the chicken. Fry the onions til golden.
3. Add the rice, rosemary, and water to the onions. Stir well. Place the chicken on top.
4. Sprinkle with salt and pepper.
5. Cover tightly. Cook over low heat 30 – 35 minutes, or til the rice is fluffy and the chicken juices run clear.

OR a 6-qt. Electric Pressure Cooker
Cooking Time: 14 minutes; 10 minutes to reduce pressure

1. Sauté the onions on Normal in 2 tablespoons butter til just brown.
2. Turn off the Sauté setting. Add the water. Stir loose any brown bits. Salt and pepper the chicken. Settle it into the broth.
3. Add the rice over top, pushing it down into the broth. Salt and pepper it. Scatter rosemary over top.
4. Pressure cook on High 12 minutes (valve closed; Keep Warm setting off).
5. Press the quick-release button. Keep the lid on, and open the pressure valve for 10 minutes.
6. Lift out the thighs. Stir the other ingredients together well; then serve with the chicken.

Chicken *Roasht*

4 - 6 servings

Prep Time: 15 - 30 minutes, depending on whether you're deboning a chicken

- ¾ stick (6 tablespoons) butter, melted
- ⅔ cup chopped onions

- ¾ teaspoon salt and ¼ teaspoon black pepper
- 6 – 7 cups sturdy bread cubes
- 3 cups cut-up cooked chicken
- 2 – 3 cups water

6-qt. Slow Cooker
Cooking Time: 3 - 4 hours

1. Grease the interior of a 5- or 6-quart slow cooker crock.

2. Fold all ingredients together in a large bowl. Spoon into the crock.

3. Cover. Cook on Low 3 – 4 hours, or until hot through.

Optional ingredients:

1. Add any or all of these to Step 2: 1 cup chopped celery, 2 beaten eggs, 1 teaspoon baking powder for added flavor and lightness.

2. Substitute 2 – 3 cups organic chicken broth for the water.

3. Use cooked turkey instead of chicken.

OR an Oven
Roasting Time: 30 - 60 minutes

1. Preheat the oven to 350°.

2. Fold all ingredients together in a big bowl. Spoon the mixture into a large roasting pan.

3. Cover with a lid or foil. Roast 30 – 60 minutes, or until hot through. To increase browning, remove the lid or foil during the last 20 minutes. (Watch to make sure it doesn't dry out or over-brown.)

This is the traditional dish served at the big meal following an Amish wedding. The wedding and the meal are both held at the home of the bride and often include several hundred guests. (No, the food is not catered!)

Lime Chicken Tacos

4 - 5 servings   **Prep Time: 10 minutes**   *from Kim L.*

- juice and zest of 1 big, or 2 small, limes
- 2 garlic cloves, minced
- 1 teaspoon dried oregano

- salt and pepper to taste
- 2 - 3 tablespoons water
- 2 pounds boneless skinless chicken thighs

4- or 5-qt. Slow Cooker
Cooking Time: 3 - 4 hours

1. Place all ingredients except the thighs in the crock. Mix well.

2. Lay the thighs in one-by-one, coating well with the sauce.

3. Cover. Cook on Low 3 – 4 hours, or until the meat is tender but not dry.

4. Shred the chicken with two forks in a bowl. (Keep the broth warm in the covered crock.)

5. Spoon ½ cup broth from the cooker into the shredded meat. Stir, adding more broth if you want. Taste. Add more seasoning if needed.

Optional ingredients:

Add 2 tablespoons red wine vinegar and 1 teaspoon cumin in Step 1.

OR a 6-qt. Electric Pressure Cooker
Cooking Time: 8 minutes; 20 minutes to reduce pressure naturally

1. Pour 1 cup water and flavorings into the crock. Add the wire rack and thighs.

2. Pressure cook on High 8 minutes (valve closed; Keep Warm setting off).

3. Release pressure naturally; 20 minutes. Follow Steps 4 and 5 above.

Tip:

Serve in tortillas with black beans, minced jalapeño, cubed avocado, chopped tomatoes, sautéed onion and/or bell pepper slices, grated cheese, cilantro, and sour cream. Or serve over cooked rice or quinoa with your favorite toppings.

Dressed Up Chicken

4 - 6 servings   ***Prep Time: 10 minutes***   *from Meredith M.*

- 6 or 7 boneless, skinless chicken thighs, each 5 – 6 ounces, seasoned
- 1 batch MIY Cheddar Sauce (recipe on page 201)

- ⅓ cup white wine
- MIY Croutons (recipe on page 214)
- half a stick (4 tablespoons) butter, melted

4- or 5-qt. Slow Cooker
Cooking Time: 4 hours

1. Place chicken thighs in the crock.
2. In a small bowl, mix together the Sauce and wine. Spread over the chicken.
3. Top with croutons and drizzle with butter.
4. Cook on High 4 hours, or until the chicken registers 160° on an instant-read meat thermometer.

OR an Oven
Roasting Time: 35 - 40 minutes

1. Preheat the oven to 425°. Grease a sheet pan. Lay thighs on it in a single layer, allowing space between them.
2. Follow Steps 2 and 3 above.
3. Roast 35 – 40 minutes, or just until the chicken is browning and registers 160° on an instant-read meat thermometer.

Herby Turkey Breast

5 - 6 servings　　　　**Prep Time: 10 minutes**　　　　**from Kim L.**

- 5 – 6-pound turkey breast, bone-in
- ¼ cup olive oil
- 3 cloves garlic, minced

- 1 teaspoon dried rosemary
- 1 teaspoon salt and ½ teaspoon coarsely ground black pepper

Oven
Roasting Time: 2 hours

1. Preheat the oven to 325°. Mix together the oil, garlic, rosemary, salt, and pepper. Loosen the skin and brush ⅓ of the oil mixture between the meat and skin.

2. Place the breast in a heavy roaster or baking pan. Cover it.

3. Bake one hour, basting the outside of the turkey with the remaining oil mixture every 15 minutes.

4. Uncover. Bake one more hour, continuing to baste every 15 minutes.

5. The meat is done when an instant-read meat thermometer inserted into the center of the breast (avoiding the bone) registers 155 – 160°. Remove the turkey from the heat. Tent with foil 10 – 15 minutes so it regathers its juices.

6. Carve, drizzle with pan drippings, and serve.

OR a 6-qt. Electric Pressure Cooker
Cooking Time: 30 - 35 minutes; 30 - 60 minutes to release pressure naturally

1. Put the wire rack in the cooker. Pour in 2 cups water or broth. Follow Step 1 above (oiling the breast). Set on rack.

2. Pressure cook on High 30 – 35 minutes, about 6 minutes per pound (valve closed; Keep Warm setting off).

3. Let the pressure release naturally, 30 – 60 minutes. Follow Steps 5 and 6 above.

4. For crispy skin, broil the cooked breast, but watch carefully so it doesn't get too dark or dry.

There is no doubt that you have to be intentional to cook weeknight meals regularly. But when you do, you join a community of home cooks who've learned that there is nothing like home-prepared food eaten each day in the presence of the people you love. So keep it simple enough that you can keep on doing it!

BEEF,
PORK,
LAMB, &
SEAFOOD

Flank Steak with a 5-Ingredient Marinade

4 servings   *Prep Time: 10 minutes*   *Marinating Time: 6 - 8 hours, or overnight*

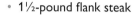

- 1½-pound flank steak
- ¼ cup chopped onions
- 2 tablespoons fresh parsley

- 2 tablespoons balsamic vinegar
- 1 tablespoon olive oil
- 2 teaspoons organic Dijon mustard

 Grill

Grilling Time: 4 - 8 minutes, or longer for more well-done meat

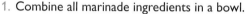

1. Combine all marinade ingredients in a bowl.
2. Place the meat in a sturdy plastic bag. Pour in the marinade and close the bag tightly. Flip the bag over several times so the meat is fully immersed in the marinade.
3. Place the filled bag in a long dish in case of any leaks. Refrigerate 6 – 8 hours, or overnight. Turn the bag over at least once during this time.
4. Heat half the grill to a high, direct heat, and the other side to a low, indirect heat.
5. Place the meat on the hottest part of the grill. Salt and pepper the side facing up, grilling 1 – 2 minutes.
6. Flip the meat over. Salt and pepper. Grill 1 – 2 minutes.
7. Move to the lower heat. Cover. Cook 1 – 2 minutes on each side.
8. Use an instant-read meat thermometer to check when the steak is done—and not overdone! Rare: 120 – 125°. Medium rare: 130 – 140°. Medium: 145°.
9. Take the steak off the grill. Rest 10 – 15 minutes, covered with foil.
10. Cut it in fairly thin slices across the grain at a sharp angle to break the meat's tough muscle fibers.

 OR a Broiler

Broiling Time: 4 - 8 minutes

1. Follow Steps 1 – 3 above.
2. Place the oven rack about 5 inches below the heat. Turn the broiler to High.
3. Set a roasting rack in a rimmed sheet pan. Lay the steak on the rack. Salt and pepper.
4. Broil 1 – 2 minutes. Flip the meat. Salt and pepper. Broil another 1 – 2 minutes.
5. Move the rack away from the direct flame. Cook 1 – 2 minutes on each side.
6. Follow Steps 8 – 10 above.

Pork, Chicken, or Beef Adobo

4 - 5 servings **Prep Time: 15 minutes, if sauce is ready**

- 1½ pounds fresh pork shoulder, cubed; *or* cut up boneless chicken thighs; *or* beef chuck roast, cubed

- 1–1½ cups Adobo Sauce (see recipe on page 194)
- 2 tablespoons cooking oil

Stove Top
Cooking Time: 40 - 70 minutes, depending on the meat

1. If using pork or chicken, cover and simmer in the Sauce 30–60 minutes, or just til tender. For beef, simmer an hour, covered, or just til tender.

2. Drain off the sauce and reserve it. Brown the meat in 2 tablespoons oil over high heat in a large skillet. (Don't crowd it.) This is to put a brown finish on the meat, not cook it more. Spoon the meat into a serving dish.

3. Pour the Adobo Sauce into the skillet. Stir loose all the browned bits and mix them into the Sauce. Pour over the meat. Serve over rice.

Optional ingredients:

Add a cut up carrot, 2 medium potatoes, 1 onion, a cup of green beans, and 2–3 cabbage leaves in step 1.

OR a 6-qt. Electric Pressure Cooker
Cooking Time: 20 - 35 minutes; 20 minutes to reduce pressure naturally

1. Sauté the meat in oil on Medium for about 5 minutes. Do it in batches.

2. Spoon the browned meat into the serving dish. Pour the Adobo Sauce into the crock. Stir loose any browned bits. Turn off the Sauté function.

3. Put the meat and its juices back into the Sauce in the cooker. Pressure cook pork or chicken on High 16 minutes (valve closed; Keep Warm setting off), or beef cubes on High 20 minutes.

4. If you're adding vegetables, first pressure-cook the meat 6 minutes on High. Reduce the pressure with quick release; stir in the vegetables. Pressure-cook 10 more minutes on High.

5. Reduce the pressure naturally. Serve over rice.

Easy Amazing Beef Curry

4 - 6 servings   **Prep Time: 20 minutes**

- 1 cup chopped onions

- 4–6 green *or* red chili peppers, seeded and minced

- 1 tablespoon curry powder, *or* MIY Garam Masala Seasoning (recipe on page 212)

- 2 tablespoons water

- 2–3-pound chuck roast

- 6 cups chopped fresh tomatoes, *or* 48 ounces organic diced, canned tomatoes

5- or 6-qt. Slow Cooker
Cooking Time: 7 - 8 hours

1. Put chopped onions, minced chili peppers, curry powder, and water into the crock. Mix well.

2. Swirl the roast through the sauce, making sure all sides are coated.

3. Settle the meat into the sauce. Top it with chopped tomatoes.

4. Cover. Cook on Low 7–8 hours, or til the meat is tender and starting to fall apart.

5. Pull the meat into chunks. Mix it through the sauce.

6. Serve over rice or with chapatis.

OR a 6- or 8-qt. Electric Pressure Cooker
Cooking Time: 40 minutes; 30 minutes to release pressure naturally

1. Mix the onions, peppers, curry powder, water, and tomatoes in the crock.

2. Cut the beef into 2-inch chunks. Stir into the vegetables and seasoning.

3. Pressure cook on High 40 minutes (valve closed; Keep Warm setting off).

4. Reduce the pressure naturally, about 30 minutes.

5. Stir meat and sauce together before serving.

Caramelized Pork Bowls

4 servings   **Prep Time: 5 minutes**   *from Kim M.*

- ½ cup MIY Spicy Onion-Garlic-Ginger Base (see recipe on page 192)
- 1 pound ground pork

- rice or rice noodles for serving

- 3 tablespoons brown sugar
- 2 tablespoons organic soy sauce *or* fish sauce

Stove Top
Cooking Time: 15 minutes

1. Warm MIY Spicy Onion-Garlic-Ginger Base in a skillet over medium heat. Add pork and cook 3 minutes, breaking up the meat as it cooks.

2. Stir in sugar and either soy sauce or fish sauce. Cook without stirring until the liquid evaporates and the pork begins to caramelize.

3. Then stir a few times, allowing the meat to caramelize as much as you want. Just make sure it doesn't dry out or scorch.

4. Serve over rice or rice noodles.

5. Top with shredded lettuce, coarsely grated carrots, and chopped green onions. Or an egg fried over easy.

Optional ingredients:

Just before serving, stir 1 teaspoon toasted sesame oil into the caramelized pork. Chopped cilantro and/or fresh mint add good flavor and color, too.

OR an Oven
Roasting Time: 3 - 13 minutes, depending on how well cooked you like it.

1. Preheat the oven to 375°. Stir the first 4 ingredients together. Spread over a lightly greased sheet pan.

2. Roast 8 – 10 minutes. Or broil 3 minutes. Stir. If still pink, roast another 2 – 3 minutes. Or broil another 1 minute.

3. Serve, along with any toppings (above) you'd like.

Grill-Pan or Skillet Burgers

4 servings **Prep Time: 2 minutes**

- 1½ pounds 80% lean ground beef
- coarse salt and pepper

- cheese slices
- buns or bread
- Pickled Pink Onions

Stove Top
Cooking Time: 4 - 6 minutes for rare; 7 for medium-rare; 8 for medium

1. Heat the grill pan or skillet til it's screaming hot.

2. On a cutting board or platter, push the ground beef into 4 separate mounds, handling the meat as little as possible. Lift each mound onto the hot pan. Salt and pepper each one.

3. Grill over high heat 2 – 3 minutes.

4. Flip with a metal spatula. If you want cheese, lay the slices on now. Grill another 2 – 3 minutes or til the burgers are charred on the outside and the inside is as rare or as well-done as you like.

5. Lift onto toasted bread or buns. Top them with Pickled Pink Onions (recipe on page 137)!

OR a Grill
Grilling Time: 4 - 7 minutes, depending on how you well cooked you like them

1. Heat a gas grill to 450 – 500°. Or a charcoal grill with high heat for 15 – 20 minutes.

2. Follow the Steps above, lifting the burger mounds onto a grill instead of a pan.

3. Rare burgers will need about 2 minutes per side; medium-rare about 2½ minutes per side; medium about 3 – 3½ minutes per side.

4. Follow Steps 4 and 5 above.

Tips:

1. Ground beef holds together better if it's cold, so keep the meat refrigerated til you're ready to form it into mounds.

2. Don't press down on the burgers while they're cooking. You'll send juice out of the meat and into the pan or grill.

Savory Roast Beef Stew

6 - 8 servings   **Prep Time: 15 minutes**   *from Regina M.*

- 2 pounds beef chuck roast, cut into 1½-inch cubes

- 4 medium carrots, peeled and cut into 1-inch cubes, *or* 1 pound baby carrots

- 1 medium to large onion, peeled and cut into chunks

- 1½ teaspoons salt and ½ teaspoon pepper

- 2 cups crushed tomatoes, fresh *or* organic canned

- ½ cup water

Oven
Roasting Time: 2 hours

1. Combine all ingredients in a Dutch oven.

2. Cover. Roast at 375° for 2 hours.

Optional ingredients:

- 2 – 3 cups fresh *or* frozen green beans

- 7 halved baby potatoes, *or* 4 medium, cubed

- ¾ cup red wine

- 2 tablespoons fresh rosemary, *or* 2 teaspoons dried

- ½ cup raisins, dried apples, dried pears, dried apricots, dried plums, *or* dried figs

Add any or all to the Dutch oven in Step 1.

OR a 6-qt. Electric Pressure Cooker
Cooking Time: 67 - 70 minutes; 30 minutes to reduce pressure naturally

1. Sauté the cubed beef in 2 tablespoons oil for about 10 minutes, or til it's as browned as you like.

2. Pressure cook on High 50 minutes (valve closed; Keep Warm setting off).

3. Reduce the pressure naturally, about 30 minutes.

4. Stir in the remaining ingredients, including as many of the optional ones as you want.

5. Pressure cook on High 7 minutes (valve closed; Keep Warm setting off).

6. Reduce the pressure naturally, about 30 minutes.

7. Taste. Adjust seasonings if needed.

Crinkly Kale with Potatoes and Smoky Sausage

4 - 6 servings   **Prep Time: 20 minutes**

- 6 – 7 potatoes, unpeeled or peeled, chunked, about 2 pounds total
- 2 – 3 tablespoons oil *or* butter, *divided*

- 1½ pounds smoked sausage, pricked with a sharp fork, then cut into 2-inch lengths
- 1 pound kale, stems stripped off and leaves chopped
- ¾ – 1 cup milk

Oven
Roasting Time: 35 - 45 minutes

1. Preheat the oven to 425°. Grease a rimmed sheet pan.
2. Place the chunked potatoes on the pan. Drizzle with half the oil. Toss.
3. Roast 18 – 22 minutes, or until the potatoes are nearly soft.
4. Add the kale and remaining oil. Toss til the kale, oil, and potatoes are well mixed. Pull the mixture to one side of the pan.
5. Spread the pricked sausage pieces in one layer on the open section.
6. Return to the oven. Continue roasting til the potatoes and kale are soft, and the sausage is browned.
7. Near the end of the roasting, warm the milk just til scalding (not boiling).
8. Mash the potatoes, kale, and hot milk together.
9. Pile onto a big platter, or back onto the sheet pan. Surround by the sausage pieces and serve.

OR a 6-qt. Electric Pressure Cooker
Cooking Time: 15 minutes; 20 minutes to reduce pressure naturally

1. Place the potatoes, 1½ tablespoons oil, and 1 cup water in the crock.
2. Pressure cook on High 5 minutes (valve closed; Keep Warm setting off).
3. Quick-release the pressure.
4. Stir in the kale. Pressure-cook on High 5 more minutes (valve closed; Keep Warm setting off).
5. Reduce the pressure naturally, about 20 minutes.
6. While the pressure is reducing, warm the milk.
7. Mash the potatoes, kale, and heated milk together.
8. Mix the sausage pieces in the crock with the remaining oil. Sauté on Normal 5 minutes.
9. Follow Step 9.

North Carolina Barbecue

8 - 12 servings   *Prep Time: 10 minutes*   *from JB M.*

- 3 – 4-pound bone-in Boston Butt, pork roast, *or* shoulder
- 1 cup cider vinegar
- 5 tablespoons organic yellow mustard
- 5 tablespoons organic Worcestershire sauce
- 2 teaspoons red pepper flakes, *optional*

5- or 6-qt. Slow Cooker
Cooking Time: 5 - 8 hours

1. Trim fat from pork. Place in the slow cooker crock.
2. Mix the remaining ingredients in a small bowl, then pour over the pork.
3. Cover. Cook on High 5 hours, or on Low 8 hours, or until the meat can be pulled apart easily with two forks.
4. Shred the tender meat on a cutting board. Then stir it back into the sauce.
5. Serve on buns or over mashed potatoes, pasta, cooked whole grains, or rice.

OR a 6-qt. Electric Pressure Cooker
Cooking Time: 95 - 100 minutes; 30 minutes to reduce pressure naturally

1. Place the meat in the cooker. Follow Step 2 above.
2. Pressure cook on High 1 hour and 30 minutes (valve closed; Keep Warm setting off).
3. Reduce the pressure naturally, about 30 minutes.
4. Shred the tender meat on a cutting board using 2 forks.
5. Meanwhile, turn the cooker to Sauté and let the sauce simmer until thickened, about 5 – 10 minutes. Stir now and then so it doesn't scorch.
6. Stir the shredded meat back into the sauce.
7. Follow Step 5 above.

Tip:

This makes a great sandwich, either topped with Cole Slaw (see recipe on page 55) or served alongside.

Ham, Green Beans, and Potatoes

4 – 5 servings   ***Prep Time: 15 minutes***

- 2 – 3-pound ham shoulder *or* picnic, *or* 2-pound meaty ham hock
- ½ cup water

- 4 good-sized potatoes, peeled or not, and chunked
- 1 pound fresh green beans, *or* 1½ pounds frozen green beans
- salt and pepper to taste

Oven
Roasting Time: 1 – 1½ hours

1. Preheat the oven to 350°.
2. Place the ham in a roaster, add water, and cover.
3. Roast 1 – 1½ hours.
4. Add potatoes and green beans to roaster.
5. Cover. Return to oven and bake another hour, or until the meat is tender and the potatoes and beans are as tender as you like them.
6. Taste. Add seasonings as needed. Cut up the meat and serve all together.

OR a 5- or 6-qt. Slow Cooker
Cooking Time: 6 - 8 hours

1. Put ham into the crock.
2. Stack the potato chunks and green beans around it.
3. Pour in ½ cup water.
4. Cover. Cook on Low 6 – 8 hours, or til everything is as tender as you like it.
5. Follow Step 6 above.

We love this served with Cole Slaw (recipe on page 55). The sweet-sour dressing and crunch of the cabbage makes the salad a great partner to this main dish.

Maple-Soy Glazed Salmon

4 servings   *Prep Time: 10 minutes*   *from Joanna R-McD.*

- 4 salmon fillets (skin on), about 5 ounces each
- 2 tablespoons organic soy sauce

- 2 tablespoons maple syrup
- 1 teaspoon minced garlic
- 1 teaspoon minced fresh ginger

 Oven
Roasting Time: 12 - 15 minutes

1. Preheat the oven to 375°.
2. Place salmon in a greased baking dish, skin side down.
3. Mix other ingredients in a small bowl. Spoon or brush them over the salmon.
4. Bake uncovered just until the fish flakes with a fork, 12–15 minutes, depending on the thickness of the pieces.

 OR a Grill
Grilling Time: 8 minutes

1. Grease the grill. (Use coals, a gas grill, or a grill pan.) Bring it to medium heat.
2. While the grill heats, brush salmon on both sides with the topping.
3. Place the salmon on the heated grill. Cover. Grill about 4 minutes on each side, depending on how thick the pieces are, just until the fish flakes with a twist of a fork.

Tip:

Serve with rice, preferably jasmine. Fresh green beans go well with it, too.

Homesteaders' One-Dish Dinner

6 - 8 servings   ***Prep Time: 20 - 30 minutes***   *from Judith R-S.*

- 2 – 3 apples, peeled or not, sliced or diced
- half a medium head of cabbage, coarsely shredded
- 2 onions, sliced

- 1 or 2 ham hocks, *or* one meaty ham bone, *or* 2 cups diced smoked or cooked ham
- salt and pepper to taste (some smoked or cooked pork may already have enough salt)

5- or 6-qt. Slow Cooker
Cooking Time: 4 - 10 hours

1. Layer the ingredients into the crock in the order given. Vary the proportion of the ingredients according to what you have on hand and what the people you'll be feeding like.

2. Cover. Cook on High 4 – 5 hours, or on Low 8 – 10 hours.

OR a Stove Top
Cooking Time: 1½ - 2½ hours

1. Sometimes I put all the ingredients inside a whole, hollowed-out pumpkin.

2. I place the pumpkin in a large stockpot and add about an inch of water.

3. I bring it to a boil and simmer until it's done, usually 1 – 2 hours.

4. Delicious! And it's fun to serve it from the pumpkin.

Stove-Top Tip:

If you don't have or want a pumpkin, layer the ingredients into a Dutch oven. Add about an inch of water. Cover. Follow Step 3 above for cooking it on a stove-top.

Tip:

We also like this dinner served over mashed potatoes.

Pork and Sweet Kraut

6 - 8 servings　　　　*Prep Time: 10 - 15 minutes*

- 4- to 4½-pound bone-in Boston butt pork roast
- salt and pepper to taste
- water

- 2 27½-ounce cans organic sauerkraut
- 4 – 6 tablespoons brown sugar
- 2 tart apples, unpeeled, cored, and sliced thin

 Oven
Roasting Time: 2¾ hours

1. Preheat the oven to 350°. Salt and pepper the meat on all sides. Place in a good-sized roasting pan, ideally with a lid. (Or cover tightly with foil.) Add water to a depth of ½ – 1 inch (up to the first knuckle of your pointer finger).

2. Cover. Roast 1¼ hours.

3. Spread sauerkraut over the pork roast. Sprinkle with brown sugar. Cover with apple slices.

4. Cover and continue roasting 1½ more hours.

5. Trim the meat of excess fat. Slice or chunk the meat and serve it alongside or mixed into the sweet kraut.

Optional ingredient:

- Add ¼ – ½ cup chopped onions in Step 3 above.

Tips:

1. Serve with mashed or roasted potatoes.

2. Serve with cold applesauce to balance the rich food.

 OR a 6- or 7-qt. Slow Cooker
Cooking Time: 4 - 5 hours

1. Season the roast and put it into the cooker. Cover it with sauerkraut and its juice. Top with brown sugar and apple slices.

2. Cook on High 4 – 5 hours.

3. Pick up with Step 5 above.

Lamb Chops Singers Glen

4 servings **Prep Time: 15 minutes** **from Robert M.**
Marinating time: 1 hour

- 8 thick-cut lamb loin chops, seasoned with Kosher salt and coarse black pepper

Marinade:

- juice of 1 lemon
- 1 tablespoon olive oil
- 3 tablespoons organic soy sauce

- 1 teaspoon light brown sugar
- 2 tablespoons chopped fresh rosemary (This is a lot of rosemary, and yes, it's worth it!)

Grill
Grilling Time: 18 minutes

1. Trim excess fat off the chops to prevent a fire in the grill. But keep enough around the edges for good flavor. Season the chops to taste. Set aside while preparing the marinade.

2. Whisk together the marinade ingredients.

3. Submerge the chops in the marinade in a single layer. Cover and refrigerate 30 minutes.

4. Remove the chops from the fridge so they can approach room temperature and continue marinating for another 30 minutes.

5. Fire up your grill on High.

6. Sear the chops over direct high heat for 3 minutes per side. Continue grilling over indirect medium heat for 6 minutes per side.

7. Remove the chops from the grill to a platter and tent with foil. Let the chops stand 6 minutes or so before serving, usually 2 chops for each person.

Tip:

Lamb loin chops look like small, thick T-bone steaks. Rack of lamb works well with this marinade, too.

SIDE
DISHES

Green Bean Tomato Toss

4 servings   *Prep Time: 15 to 20 minutes*   *from Regina M.*

- 1–1½ pounds fresh green beans, stemmed
- 4 cups halved grape tomatoes

- 2 garlic cloves, minced
- sea salt and coarsely ground pepper to taste
- 2 tablespoons oil

 Oven
Roasting Time: 15 minutes

1. Drop the beans into a large pot of boiling water. Blanche for 2 minutes, or just til crisp-tender. Empty into a sink full of cold water to stop the cooking.

2. Using tongs, shake the water off the beans. Divide them between two baking sheets, along with the grape tomatoes.

3. Sprinkle garlic, salt, and pepper over each tray.

4. Drizzle with oil and toss with your hands. (Messy? Yes. Does it do the job thoroughly, without having the vegs jump off the baking sheets? Yes.)

5. Roast at 400° 15 minutes, or until the beans are as tender as you like them.

Optional ingredients:

1 large shallot, chopped, to add in Step 3; 2 tablespoons fresh parsley and 1 handful of fresh basil, chopped, to add just before serving

 OR a Grill
Grilling Time: 4 minutes

1. Preheat the grill to 400°.

2. Put all ingredients except the optional herbs into a large bowl and toss together til well mixed.

3. Place in a grill basket. (Depending on the size of your basket, you may have to grill in batches.) Put on the grill and close the lid.

4. Grill 4 minutes, tossing the vegs a few times. You want to prevent burning but encourage overall light charring.

Note:

Delicious served hot, at room temperature, or even cold.

Garlicky Lemon Green Beans

2 - 4 servings **Prep Time: 10 minutes**

- 2 or more garlic cloves, minced
- 2 teaspoons olive oil
- 1 pound fresh green beans, whole or cut in pieces

- 1 tablespoon lemon zest and 1 tablespoon fresh lemon juice
- ¼ teaspoon salt and ¼ teaspoon coarsely ground black pepper

Stove Top
Cooking Time: 10 - 13 minutes

1. In a large skillet, sauté the garlic in oil over medium heat for half a minute.
2. Add the green beans to the skillet. Cook uncovered over medium-high heat, stirring often til the beans are as crisp-tender as you like them.
3. Scatter in the lemon zest, add the lemon juice, and sprinkle with salt and pepper. Stir til well coated.

OR an Oven
Roasting Time: 20 - 25 minutes

1. Preheat the oven to 400°.
2. Make sure the beans are fully dry. Spread in a single layer on a rimmed sheet pan.
3. Drizzle them with olive oil and lemon juice. Scatter the minced garlic, lemon zest, salt, and pepper over top. Mix everything together well with your hands.
4. Roast 20 – 25 minutes, or til the beans are crisp-tender.

Broiled Eggplant with Fresh Tomatoes, Basil, and Cheese

2 - 6 servings   *Prep Time: 15 minutes*

- 1 eggplant, peeled or not
- olive oil

- fresh tomatoes
- fresh mozzarella cheese
- fresh basil

 Broil
Broiling Time: 7 - 8 minutes

1. Cut the eggplant into ½"-thick slices. Brush each slice on both sides with olive oil. Lay on a rimmed baking sheet.
2. Broil each side til golden brown, about 3 minutes on each side.
3. Top each eggplant round with fresh tomato slices, fresh basil, and a slice of cheese.
4. Broil 1 – 2 minutes, or until the cheese melts. Watch carefully to prevent burning!

Optional ingredients and tips:

1. Sprinkle the broiled eggplant slices with salt. Drizzle the tomato slices with balsamic vinegar.
2. Use whatever cheese you prefer or have on hand. It will still be delicious!

 OR a Grill
Grilling Time: 4 - 5 minutes

1. Preheat the grill to 400°.
2. Follow Steps 1 and 2, except lay the eggplant slices across the hot grill.
3. Grill each side til golden brown, about 2 minutes per side.
4. Follow Step 3 above. Then return to the grill just till the cheese melts from the heat.

Completely YUM!

Blistered Asparagus

4 servings **Prep Time: 10 minutes**

- 1½ pounds fresh asparagus
- 3 tablespoons olive oil
- 2 teaspoons sesame oil

- ¼ teaspoon salt and ¼ teaspoon coarsely ground black pepper
- 2–3 tablespoons sesame seeds

Oven
Roasting Time: 10 minutes

1. Preheat the oven to 400°.
2. Lay the asparagus, full-length or cut, on an ungreased rimmed baking sheet.
3. Combine the olive and sesame oils and drizzle them over the asparagus.
4. Sprinkle with salt and pepper. Shake the tray so the asparagus rolls and gets covered on all sides.
5. Roast 10 minutes, or until the asparagus is as tender as you like.
6. Toast the sesame seeds in a dry skillet over medium heat as the asparagus roasts. Stir continually until the seeds turn golden brown.
7. Sprinkle seeds over the roasted asparagus just before serving.

Optional ingredient:

Add 1 tablespoon balsamic vinegar to the oils in Step 3 before drizzling over the asparagus.

OR a Grill
Grilling Time: 3 - 4 minutes

1. Preheat the grill to 400°.
2. Put all the ingredients except the seeds in a large bowl and toss together til well mixed.
3. Place in a grill basket. (Depending on the size of your basket, you may have to grill in batches.) Put on the grill and close the lid.
4. Grill 4 minutes, tossing the vegs a few times. You want to prevent burning but encourage overall light charring.
5. Follow Steps 6 and 7 above.

Peach-Glazed Fresh Carrots

6 - 8 servings   **Prep Time: 5 - 15 minutes**

- 2 pounds fresh carrots
- water
- ⅔ cup organic peach preserves
- ¼ stick (2 tablespoons) butter
- salt and coarsely ground black pepper

 Stove Top
Cooking Time: 10 - 15 minutes

1. Slice the carrots. Cook in a small amount of water in a covered saucepan over medium-high heat til they're as crisp-tender as you like, 10 – 15 minutes.
2. Drain off the water but keep the carrots in the pan.
3. Stir in the peach preserves and butter. Warm over low heat so the preserves and butter melt. Mix well through the carrot slices.
4. Taste. Sprinkle with salt and pepper as you like, and serve.

 OR a 6-qt. Electric Pressure Cooker
Cooking Time: 5 - 6 minutes; quick-release pressure

1. Slice the carrots. Pour 2 cups of water in the crock. Add the carrots.
2. Pressure cook on High 3 minutes (valve closed; Keep Warm setting off).
3. Quick-release the pressure.
4. Drain the carrots in a colander. Discard the cooking water.
5. Sauté the preserves and butter in the cooker on Medium, 2 – 3 minutes, or til both have melted.
6. Place the carrots in a serving dish. Pour the glaze over top. Sprinkle with salt and pepper if needed, toss, and then serve.

Sesame Broccoli

4 - 5 servings   **Prep Time: 10 minutes**

- 1 large head fresh broccoli, about 6–8 cups
- 1 teaspoon olive oil
- 1 tablespoon sesame seeds

- 2 tablespoons water
- 1 tablespoon organic soy sauce
- 1½ teaspoons fresh lemon juice

Stove Top
Cooking Time: 10 minutes

1. Cut up the florets. Peel the broccoli stalks. Cut them into small chunks.
2. Heat a large skillet over medium-high heat. Add oil and tilt to coat the bottom.
3. Stir in the sesame seeds. Cook one minute, stirring continually. Remove the toasted seeds.
4. Stir in the broccoli pieces. Increase the heat to high. Cook 3 minutes, stirring continually until the broccoli becomes bright green.
5. Stir in the soy sauce and lemon juice. Cover the skillet. Reduce the heat to medium. Cook 5 minutes, or until the broccoli becomes crisp-tender.
6. Sprinkle with the seeds and serve.

OR an Oven
Roasting Time: about 15 - 20 minutes

1. Preheat the oven to 450°.
2. Increase the oil to 1 tablespoon. Mix it, the cut-up broccoli, soy sauce, and lemon juice together.
3. Pour onto a rimmed baking sheet, spreading it into a single layer.
4. Place on the bottom oven rack. Roast til it's as tender as you like, about 15–20 minutes. Sprinkle with seeds and serve.

Hasselback Z's

4 servings **Prep Time: 15 minutes**

- 2 medium zucchinis, each about 6 inches long
- 2 teaspoons olive oil
- ¼ teaspoon garlic powder

- 1 – 2 teaspoons finely minced onions
- ¼ cup grated Parmesan cheese

Oven
Baking Time: 30 - 35 minutes

1. Preheat the oven to 375°.

2. Trim the ends off the zucchinis. Make a cross-cut into the zucchinis at about every half inch, but don't cut the whole through. You want whole zucchinis; not lots of pieces.

3. Place each zucchini on a piece of foil, large enough to wrap it completely.

4. Drizzle each one with olive oil. Sprinkle with garlic powder; scatter the minced onions over top.

5. Wrap without disturbing the toppings. Pinch closed. Lay on a rimmed baking sheet.

6. Bake 30 – 35 minutes, or til tender when poked with a fork.

7. Open the foil and scatter cheese over top.

8. Return to the oven for 1 – 2 minutes, or til the cheese has melted.

OR a Microwave
Cooking Time: 3 - 5 minutes

1. Follow Step 2.

2. Lay the zucchinis on a microwave-safe plate or shallow dish. Follow Step 4.

3. Sprinkle each Z with Parm cheese.

4. Cover with a microwave-safe domed lid or plastic wrap laid on loosely.

5. Mic on High 3 minutes. Poke with a fork. If they're tender, you're done; if they're not, mic another 2 – 3 minutes. Stop before the Z's fall in on themselves and turn mushy.

Brussels Sprouts with Cranberry Balsamic Glaze

6 servings   *Prep Time: 20 minutes*

- 2 tablespoons balsamic vinegar
- 1 tablespoon water
- 3 tablespoons olive oil
- ¼ teaspoon salt

- 2 pounds fresh or frozen Brussels sprouts, trimmed and halved
- ¼ cup dried cranberries, coarsely chopped

Stove Top
Cooking Time: 8–10 minutes

1. Combine the vinegar, water, oil, and salt in a blender or food processor. Pulse til well combined. Set aside.

2. Use a saucepan that will accommodate a vegetable steamer. Put 2–3 inches of water in the pan. Cover and bring to a boil.

3. Place the steamer in the pan, and then the prepared sprouts.

4. Cover. Steam the sprouts 5–8 minutes, or until they're just-tender. Poke with a fork to test.

5. Lift the sprouts out of the pan. Toss them with the cranberries and then the dressing—and serve.

OR a Microwave
Cooking Time: 8–10 minutes

1. Follow Step 1.

2. Place the prepped sprouts and 2–3 tablespoons water in a microwave-safe dish. Cover, and mic on High 2 minutes. Stir. Re-cover.

3. Repeat 3 times, or more, just until the sprouts are as tender as you like them.

4. Drain off the cooking water. Then continue with Step 5.

Sautéed Cabbage

4 - 6 servings   *Prep Time: 3 minutes*   *from Susie S-W.*

- 1 medium head green cabbage
- 3 tablespoons olive oil
- salt and pepper to taste
- ½ – 1 teaspoon dried tarragon
- toasted sesame seeds

 Stove Top
Cooking Time: 8 minutes

1. Cut the cabbage in half and then in half again the other direction. Remove the white cores from each quarter and discard them. Or cut them fine and eat them raw.

2. Chop the cabbage.

3. Heat oil in a wide skillet over high heat. Stir in the chopped cabbage.

4. Sprinkle with salt and pepper. Cook over medium heat for about 8 – 10 minutes, stirring now and then.

5. When the cabbage is glossy but still has some crunch, remove it from the heat.

6. Sprinkle it with the tarragon and sesame seeds. Toss and serve.

 OR a 6-qt. Electric Pressure Cooker
Cooking Time: 8 minutes; quick-release pressure

1. Place chopped cabbage and olive oil in the cooker. Stir together well.

2. Pressure cook 8 minutes on High (valve closed; Keep Warm setting off).

3. Quick-release the pressure.

4. Follow Step 6 above.

Red Cabbage and Apples

6 servings   *Prep Time: 15 - 20 minutes*

- half a head of red cabbage
- 6 – 8 whole cloves
- ¼ cup apple cider vinegar

- 2 tart apples, peeled or not, and sliced or chopped
- 1 – 2 tablespoons brown sugar

Stove Top
Cooking Time: 30 minutes

1. Slice the cabbage. Then cut across the slices to make fairly small pieces.
2. Place in a 3- or 4-quart saucepan, along with the cloves (in a spice ball) and vinegar.
3. Cover. Cook til the cabbage is tender, about 20 minutes. Stir now and then.
4. Stir in the apples and brown sugar.
5. Cover. Cook another 10 minutes, or til the apples are softened yet not mushy.
6. Taste. Add seasoning if needed.

OR a 6-qt. Electric Pressure Cooker
Cooking Time: 12 minutes; quick-release the pressure

1. Follow Step 1 above. Put all ingredients in the crock. Stir them together well.
2. Pressure cook on High 12 minutes (valve closed; Keep Warm setting off).
3. Quick-release the pressure.
4. Taste. Add seasoning if needed.

Stuffed Sweet Potato Surprise

4 servings   *Prep Time: 20 minutes*

- 4 good-sized sweet potatoes

Sweet potato stuffing:

- ¼ stick (2 tablespoons) butter, softened
- ⅓ cup orange juice

- 1½ teaspoons salt
- 1 small ripe banana, smashed
- ¼ cup chopped pecans

Oven
Baking Time: 57–75 minutes

1. Preheat the oven to 375°. Prick each sweet potato all over with a fork 4–6 times. Rub them well with oil.
2. Bake 45–60 minutes, or til fully tender.
3. Cut each potato in half. When cool enough to handle, scoop the potato out of the shell without tearing it.
4. Put the pulp in a bowl, along with the remaining ingredients. Mix together well.
5. Spoon the mixture into the potato shells. Place them in a greased baking dish.
6. Bake 12–15 minutes. If the potatoes begin to brown too much, cover them with foil.

OR a Microwave
Cooking Time: 20 minutes

1. Prick each potato with a fork 4–6 times. Rub them well with oil.
2. Arrange them spoke-fashion on the floor of the microwave. Mic on High 16 minutes (4 minutes per potato), or til completely tender.
3. Follow Steps 3 and 4 above.
4. Spoon the mixture into the shells and place them in a microwave-safe dish.
5. Mic on High 4 minutes, or til hot through.

Sweet Potatoes and Apples

6 - 8 servings   ***Prep Time: 15 minutes***

- 4 big tart apples, cored but unpeeled
- 6 big sweet potatoes, peeled
- 1 teaspoon salt, *divided*

- half a stick (4 tablespoons), butter, *divided*
- ½ cup honey, *or* brown sugar

Oven
Baking Time: 1 hour

1. Pre-heat the oven to 350°. Grease the interior of a large baking dish or roaster.
2. Slice the apples and sweet potatoes into ½-inch-thick slices.
3. Make one layer of apples and potatoes in the baking dish, alternating slices as you go. Sprinkle with half the salt.
4. Repeat the layers.
5. Microwave the butter and honey together til smooth.
6. Spoon the sauce over the fruit and vegs.
7. Cover. Bake 1 hour, or til the potatoes are as soft as you like.

Variation:

For a fruitier flavor and thicker sauce, stir 1 − 1½ tablespoons flour and 2 − 3 tablespoons orange juice into Step 5.

OR a 4- or 5-qt. Slow Cooker
Cooking Time: 6 - 7 hours

1. Follow Steps 2 − 6 above, placing the ingredients in a slow cooker crock.
2. Cover and cook on Low 6 − 7 hours, or til the potatoes are as soft as you like.

Red Hot Sweet Potato Fries—Two Ways!

4 servings   *Prep Time: 10 - 15 minutes*

- 4 large sweet potatoes, peeled or not

Sweet Potato Seasoning:

- 2 teaspoons kosher salt
- 1 teaspoon cayenne pepper
- 3 tablespoons olive oil

- 3 tablespoons maple syrup
- ½ cup sour cream *or* yogurt

 Oven
Roasting Time: 25 minutes

1. Peel the potatoes, or don't. Preheat the oven to 400°. Cut the potatoes into matchsticks. Place them in a good-sized bowl.

2. Stir the salt, pepper, and olive oil into the potatoes. Spread them in a single layer on a greased rimmed sheet pan.

3. Roast 7 minutes. Stir. Continue roasting 15 more minutes.

4. Mix the maple syrup and sour cream. Serve as a dip.

OR ease back on the amount of cayenne pepper, skip the maple syrup-sour cream dip, and top the finished fries with *Caramelized Kimchi*.

Caramelized Kimchi
Prep Time: 5 minutes   *Stove-Top Cooking Time: 40 - 60 minutes*

- 2 cups homemade, *or* organic store-bought, kimchi
- ¼ cup brown sugar

- 2 tablespoons organic soy sauce
- 2 tablespoons apple cider vinegar

1. Cook the kimchi, brown sugar, soy sauce, and vinegar together in a non-stick skillet over medium heat. Stir til most of the liquid cooks off and the kimchi is sticky, about 40–60 minutes.

2. Spoon over the fries, along with Sriracha Mayo (recipe on page 200).

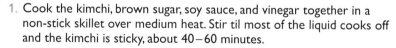

Nutty Sweets

6 - 8 servings   *Prep Time: 10 minutes*   *from Susie S-W.*

- 8–10 medium-sized orange sweet potatoes
- 2 tablespoons olive oil

- 2 tablespoons maple syrup, *or* to taste
- about one teaspoon cinnamon
- toasted and salted chopped hazelnuts

Oven
Baking Time: 30 - 40 minutes

1. Wash and scrub the sweet potatoes. Peel them, or keep the skins on for more nutrition. Cut into 1-inch chunks.

2. Pre-heat the oven to 375°. Place the sweets in a 9″ × 13″ baking dish. Coat with olive oil.

3. Roast for about 20 minutes. Stir and drizzle the maple syrup and cinnamon over top. Roast 10 more minutes or so until the potatoes jag tender.

4. Remove from the oven. Sprinkle with nuts just before serving.

Variations:

1. Choose any nuts you like. Toasted pumpkin seeds are delicious, too.

2. Lightly toast the nuts in a dry skillet. Stir occasionally so they don't burn. Add salt if you wish.

OR a 6-qt. Electric Pressure Cooker
Cooking Time: 15 minutes; 20 minutes to reduce pressure naturally

1. Place the wire rack in the bottom of the cooker. Pour in 1½ cups water. Pile in the chunked sweet potatoes.

2. Pressure cook on High 15 minutes (valve closed; Keep Warm setting off).

3. Release the pressure naturally, about 20 minutes.

4. Place the sweets in a serving dish. Stir in maple syrup and cinnamon. Sprinkle with nuts.

Tip:

Serve with Pears, Pecans, and Leafy Greens (see recipe on page 50).

Curried Mashed Potatoes

4 - 5 servings   *Prep Time: 20 minutes*

- 4 good-sized white potatoes
- ¾ cup milk, hot but not boiling

- 1 medium onion, chopped
- 2 chili peppers, seeds removed, chopped fine
- ½ teaspoon turmeric

Stove Top
Cooking Time: 20 minutes

1. Peel the potatoes and cut them into chunks. Meanwhile, bring a saucepan half-full of water to a boil.
2. Boil the potatoes til tender, 15 - 20 minutes.
3. While the potatoes cook, heat the milk to scalding.
4. Chop the onions and peppers. Sweat them in a skillet til tender.
5. When the potatoes are tender, drain them. Mash them with the hot milk slowly, til well mixed and as smooth as you want.
6. Stir in the sautéed onions, peppers, and turmeric. Taste. Add salt if needed.

OR a Microwave
Cooking Time: about 15 minutes

1. Peel and chunk the potatoes. Place them in a microwave-safe bowl. Add enough water to cover half the potatoes.
2. Cover the bowl. Microwave on High 4 minutes. Stir. Continue microwaving for 4-minute intervals, stirring between each one, until the potatoes become very soft.
3. Pour off the water and begin mashing.
4. Meanwhile, microwave the milk in a small microwave-safe container, uncovered, 2 minutes on High or just til scalded.
5. Mash milk into potatoes slowly so the milk blends in rather than flying out of the bowl.
6. Put the onions and peppers into the bowl that held the milk. Mic on High uncovered for 1½ - 2 minutes, or til softened.
7. Follow Step 6 above.

MIY Hash Browns

6 servings

Prep Time: 5 minutes
Standing Time: 2 hours
Chilling Time 4 - 6 hours

from Margaret H.

- 6 medium-size baking potatoes
- unsalted butter

4- or 5-qt. Slow Cooker
Cooking Time: 4 - 6 hours total

1. Wash and dry the potatoes. Prick each one at a few places with a sharp fork. Rub each potato all over with butter.

2. Stack them into the slow cooker. (No need to add liquid.)

3. Cover. Cook on Low 4–6 hours, or til they're cooked through but still firm in the center. Start checking if they're done after about 4 hours. If they're not, continue checking them every 30 minutes til they are.

4. Lay the cooked potatoes on wire racks in a single layer to cool. When they're room temperature (after about 2 hours), you can peel them. But I like the flavor and color the peels add to the hash browns.

5. Refrigerate 4–6 hours. That makes them easier to grate.

6. Grate the potatoes. Two-quart bags or boxes hold about 32 ounces, the usual store package size. Or use a one-quart bag to make "Sizzling Breakfast" on page 144!

7. If you've made more than you need now, label and freeze them for up to 6 months.

OR an Oven
Baking Time: 60 - 70 minutes

1. Preheat the oven to 350°. Follow Step 1 above.

2. Set the prepared potatoes right on the oven rack. Bake for 1 hour or until cooked through. Place foil or a pan on the oven rack below to catch any drips.

3. Follow Steps 4–7 above.

Coconut Rice

4 - 5 servings   *Prep Time: 5 minutes*

- 1½ cups uncooked long-grain rice
- 2½ cups (or about a whole and a half 13½-ounce cans) coconut milk

- ½ teaspoon salt
- ¼ teaspoon ground turmeric

Stove Top
Cooking Time: 20 - 25 minutes

1. Pour all ingredients into a heavy saucepan and bring to a boil.

2. Cover the pan and drop the heat so the mixture simmers gently for about 20 minutes.

3. When the rice is soft but not dried out, remove the pan from the heat. Let it stand 10 – 15 minutes to firm up before serving.

Variations:

1. If you wish, add 2 bay leaves to Step 1. Remove them before serving.

2. If it bugs you to have a partial can of coconut milk left, increase the amount of uncooked rice to 1¾ cups and use two 13½-ounce cans coconut milk. Slightly round up the salt and turmeric if you do this. Any leftover coconut rice will disappear quickly!

OR a 6-qt. Electric Pressure Cooker
Cooking Time: if using the original amounts of ingredients, 10 minutes; 15 minutes for pressure to release naturally

1. Stir all ingredients together in the crock.

2. Pressure cook on High 10 minutes (valve closed; Keep Warm setting off).

3. Reduce pressure naturally, about 15 minutes.

Pickled Pink Onions

2½ cups **Prep Time: 5 minutes** *from Kim M.*

- 1 large red onion, sliced thin
- 1 cup red wine vinegar
- 2 teaspoons balsamic vinegar

- ⅓ cup sugar
- ¼ teaspoon salt

Stove Top
Cooking Time: 5 minutes

1. Place onion slices in a canning jar or heat-proof bowl.

2. Heat the 2 vinegars, sugar, and salt in a small saucepan, stirring until the sugar dissolves.

3. Pour the hot vinegar mixture over the sliced onions. Cover and allow to cool.

Variation:

For a spicy version, add crushed chili pepper or a sliced hot pepper in Step 2 before heating the vinegar mixture.

Tips:

1. These keep well in the refrigerator.

2. Eat them as a side dish or as a topping on salads and sandwiches.

Rice from Persia

Makes 6 servings **Prep Time: 5 minutes**

- 2½ tablespoons olive oil
- 2 cups uncooked long-grain white basmati rice
- 2 cups orange juice
- 2 cups water
- 1 cup raisins
- ½ teaspoon grated orange rind

6-qt. Electric Pressure Cooker
Cooking Time: 10 - 11 minutes; 10 minutes for quick-release of pressure

1. Place the oil and rice in the crock. Sauté for a minute or so, just until the grains are well coated.
2. Turn off the Sauté function. Add all remaining ingredients to the crock except the orange rind.
3. Pressure cook 9 minutes on High (valve closed; Keep Warm setting off).
4. Quick-release the pressure with the cooker closed. Open the valve for 10 minutes.
5. Stir everything together well. Scatter grated orange rind over top before serving.

OR a Microwave
Cooking Time: 21 minutes; 5 minutes to firm up

1. Mix all ingredients except the orange rind in a microwave-safe bowl.
2. Cover tightly. Cook on High 6 minutes, or til the liquid boils.
3. Cook on Medium (power 5), covered, 15 minutes, or til nearly all of the liquid is absorbed and the rice is tender.
4. Stir in the orange rind. Let stand 5 minutes.

Tip:

This is a perfect base or side dish for Chickpea Curry (recipe on page 45) and for Braised Chicken from the East (recipe on page 83).

Fresh Corn and Zucchini Blend

4 servings   **Prep Time: 10 - 15 minutes**

- 6 slices bacon
- 4 cups unpeeled, coarsely chopped zucchini

- 3 cups fresh corn kernels
- 1 medium onion, chopped
- 1 cup shredded cheese of your choice

Stove Top
Time: 15 - 20 minutes

1. Brown bacon til crispy. Break into pieces, and set aside. Drain off all but 2 tablespoons of drippings.
2. Sauté zucchini, corn, and onion in the drippings til tender, about 10 minutes.
3. Fold in the bacon.
4. Top with shredded cheese. Run under a broiler for 1 – 2 minutes, just til the cheese melts and browns lightly.

Optional Ingredients:

Add salt and pepper to taste in Step 3.

Variation:

Drop the bacon if you wish. Sauté the vegs in coconut oil, or steam them instead.

OR an Oven
Time: 30 minutes

1. Preheat the oven to 400°. Lay the bacon slices on a rimmed sheet pan.
2. Bake 10 – 15 minutes, or til the bacon is as crispy as you like. Break into pieces and set it aside.
3. Stir the zucchini, corn, and onion into the drippings.
4. Roast 15 – 20 minutes, or til the vegs are as tender as you like them.
5. Finish with Step 4 above.

This tastes like pure summer. We love it with anything grilled. Sometimes we use it as a topping for baked potatoes.

BREAKFASTS & BRUNCHES

Santa Fe Eggs

6 servings   *Prep Time: 15 minutes*

- 9" or 10" pre-baked pie crust
- 4½ cups grated cheese—your choice of one (or a combination) that melts well and has a bit of a bite

- 6 eggs
- ¾ cup milk
- ¾ cup chopped green chilies

 Oven

Baking Time: 45 minutes; Standing Time: 10 minutes

1. Preheat the oven to 400°. To pre-bake the crust, jag it 8 times or so on its bottom and sides with a sharp fork.

2. Pre-bake it 10–12 minutes until it begins to brown. Check after 5 or 6 minutes. If the crust is bubbling up, jag the bubbles and go on baking.

3. Cover the bottom crust with cheese.

4. Beat the eggs, milk, and chilies together. Pour the mixture carefully over the cheese so you don't disturb it.

5. Bake 45 minutes, or until a knife stuck into the center comes out clean.

6. Let stand 10 minutes before slicing and serving.

Variations:

1. Add 1½ cups or so diced fresh tomatoes in Step 4.

2. Or serve the finished quiche with salsa.

 OR a 6- or 7-qt. Slow Cooker

Cooking Time: 2 hours

1. Skip the pie crust. Grease the interior of a 1½- or 2-quart baking dish that fits into your slow cooker.

2. Mix the cheese, eggs, milk and chilies together in the baking dish.

3. Set the dish on a small trivet that can withstand heat, or on metal jar rings, just so it's elevated slightly off the floor of the cooker.

4. Cover the crock. Cook on High 2 hours, or until a knife stuck into the center of the eggs comes out clean.

5. Lift the baking dish out of the cooker.

6. Follow Step 6 above.

Sizzling Breakfast

6 servings **Prep Time: 15 minutes**
(If you wish, you can mix this up and refrigerate it overnight.)

- 1 pound, *or* 3 cups, MIY Hash Browns, thawed (see recipe on page 134)
- 6 eggs

- ½ pound cooked sausage, bacon, *or* bite-sized pieces of ham
- 1 cup (4 ounces) grated cheddar cheese
- ½ cup milk

Oven
Baking Time: 1 hour

1. Preheat the oven to 350°.

2. Mix everything together. Spoon the mixture into a greased baking dish.

3. Bake uncovered for 1 hour, or until it's set and browned.

Optional Ingredients and Variations:

Add salt and pepper to taste in Step 2. And some chopped bell peppers, onions, and mushrooms in Step 2. Or already-cooked vegs. Reduce the amount of meat. Or double all the quantities; cook an additional 15–20 minutes if you do.

OR a 5- or 6-qt. Slow Cooker
Cooking Time: 3–4 hours

1. Place half the hash browns in the cooker, then half the meat.

2. Layer in the remaining hash browns, followed by the remaining meat.

3. Mix the eggs, cheese, and milk together. Pour over the layers.

4. Cover. Cook on Low 3–4 hours, or til the eggs are set in the middle.

5. Let stand 10 minutes to firm up before serving.

Cheddar-Ham Oven Omelet

9 - 10 servings   ***Prep Time: 10 minutes***

- 16 eggs
- 2 cups milk

- 2 cups (8 ounces) shredded cheddar cheese
- ¾ cup cubed fully cooked ham
- 6 green onions, chopped or sliced

Oven
Baking Time: 40 - 45 minutes; Standing Time: 10 minutes

1. Preheat the oven to 350°. Grease a 9" × 13" baking dish.

2. Beat the eggs and milk together in a good-sized bowl. Stir in the cheese, ham, and onions. Pour into the prepared baking dish.

3. Bake uncovered 40–45 minutes, or til a knife inserted into the center comes out clean.

4. Let stand 10 minutes so the eggs can set up. Then cut and serve.

Optional Ingredients and Variations:

- Add ½ teaspoon salt and ¼ teaspoon black pepper to Step 2. Add chopped bell peppers and sliced mushrooms, too, if you like.

- Substitute cooked sausage or bacon for the ham.
- Serve with prepared horseradish and/or salsa.

OR a 5- or 6-qt. Slow Cooker
Cooking Time: 2 - 3 hours

1. Find a 2-quart baking dish that fits into your slow cooker. Depending on the shape, you may need an oval cooker. Grease the interior of the baking dish. Follow Step 2 above.

2. Set the filled baking dish in the crock. Pour ½ inch of water around the baking dish. (Be careful not to get water in the egg mixture.)

3. Cover the crock. Cook on Low 2–3 hours, or until the eggs are set but not dry.

4. Use oven mitts to lift the baking dish out of the crock. Follow Step 4 above.

Write in this book—because you discover things as you cook. If you substitute an ingredient or change the cooking time, make a note on the page. Give the recipe a grade. You'll be glad you did when, in the future, you want to remember which recipes you and your family have really enjoyed.

Angel Puff

8 servings   **Prep Time: 10 minutes**   **from Kim M.**

Base:

- ½ cup flour
- 1 teaspoon baking powder
- 12 eggs
- 3 cups cottage cheese
- half a stick (¼ cup) butter, melted

Oven

Baking Time: 30 minutes

1. Preheat the oven to 350°.
2. Mix the flour and baking powder in a small bowl.
3. In a sizable bowl, beat the eggs until foamy.
4. Add the cheese, butter, and dry ingredient mixture to the eggs. Mix gently.
5. Pour into a greased 9″ × 13″ baking pan.

Toppings:

- 2–3 cups chopped fresh spinach
- 1½ cups sautéed chopped onions
- 2 cups sliced fresh *or* sautéed mushrooms
- ½–2 cups shredded cheddar cheese
- ¾ cup cooked bacon, sausage, *or* ham

1. Scatter any or all of the above over the egg mixture before baking.
2. Bake 30 minutes, or until set but not dry.

Cheesy Grits

4 - 5 servings   **Soaking Time: 8 hours, or overnight**   **Prep Time: 30 minutes**

- 3½ cups water
- 1 cup stone-ground grits
- 1 stick (8 tablespoons) butter

- 2 cups (8 ounces) sharp cheddar cheese, *divided*
- 2 eggs, beaten
- milk

4-qt. Slow Cooker
Cooking Time: 3½ hours

1. Grease the interior of the crock. Stir in the water and grits. Cover and soak 8 hours, or overnight.

2. Cut the butter into small pieces and stir them into the grits and water.

3. Cover. Cook on High 3 hours. If it looks like the grits might cook dry before they're completely tender, add ¼–½ cup water.

4. Beat the eggs and pour them into a one-cup measure. Fill the cup with milk. Stir into the grits, along with 1¾ cups cheese.

5. Cover. Cook on High 20 minutes more, or til the grits are hot and creamy and the cheese is melted.

6. Turn off the cooker. Sprinkle the remaining cheese over top. Cover and let the grits stand til the cheese melts.

OR a Stove Top
Cooking Time: 50 - 60 minutes

1. Bring the water and 1 tablespoon of butter to a boil in a 3- or 4-quart sturdy saucepan. Stir in the unsoaked grits slowly. Simmer on low.

2. Stir now and then so the grits don't cook dry. In about 15 minutes they will thicken.

3. Follow Step 4 above, but do *not* add the cheese yet. Cook over low heat, stirring now and then, for about 35 minutes. Taste to make sure the grits are fully cooked.

4. Turn off the heat. Stir in 1¾ cups of cheese. Cover. Let stand 10 minutes.

5. Scatter remaining ¼ cup cheese over top. Let it melt, and then serve.

Apple Peanut Butter Granola

8 servings   *Prep Time: 20 minutes*

- 1 stick (8 tablespoons) butter, cut into slices
- 1 cup organic natural peanut butter

- ¾ cup brown sugar
- 6 cups rolled dry oats
- ¾ cup chopped dried apples

Oven
Baking Time: 25 minutes

1. Microwave the butter, peanut butter, and brown sugar together in a microwave-safe bowl on High for 45 seconds.

2. Stir. Continue cooking for 30-second intervals, stirring in between, til the mixture is fully melted.

3. Preheat the oven to 350°.

4. Meanwhile, put the dry oats and dried apples in a very large bowl or roaster. Stir.

5. Pour the warm peanut butter mixture over top and stir til well mixed. The warmer the wet ingredients, the easier it is to mix thoroughly.

6. Spread out on a baking sheet with rims. Bake 25 minutes. If you like clumpy granola, don't stir. If you like smaller pieces, stir several times while baking.

7. Let cool. Store in an airtight container.

OR a 5- or 6-qt. Slow Cooker
Cooking Time: 1 - 2 hours

1. Follow Steps 1 and 2 above. Follow Steps 4 and 5 but mix in the greased slow cooker crock.

2. Cover, but vent the lid, using the handle of a wooden spoon or a chopstick to prop it partway open.

3. Cook on High 1 hour. Stir up from the bottom and around the sides every 20 minutes.

4. When the granola is beginning to brown and dry, pour it onto a large rimmed baking sheet to cool. Don't stir if you like clumps. Or stir into bite-sized pieces if you prefer.

5. Follow Step 7.

Grainless Granola

10 servings　　　**Prep Time: 10 minutes**　　　*from Kristina S.*

- ½ cup unsweetened flaked coconut
- 4½ cups raw unsalted nuts—slivered almonds, chopped pecans, and/or chopped walnuts

- ¼ cup flaxseed meal
- 3 tablespoons coconut oil
- ⅓ cup honey, maple syrup, *or* agave nectar

4-qt. Slow Cooker
Cooking Time: 2½ hours

1. Grease the crock. Mix coconut flakes, nuts, and flaxseed meal in the crock.
2. Place coconut oil and honey in a small sauce pan and melt over low heat, stirring to combine. Pour over the dry mixture and stir until evenly coated.
3. Cover, but vent the lid, using the handle of a wooden spoon or a chopstick to prop it partway open. That will allow steam to escape.
4. Cook on High 2½ hours.
5. When the granola is lightly browned, spread it out on a baking sheet to cool completely.
6. Store in an airtight container for up to one week.

Optional Ingredients

- Add 1 teaspoon salt in Step 1.
- Stir in 1 teaspoon vanilla and/or 1 teaspoon cinnamon in Step 2.

OR an Oven
Baking Time: 15–17 minutes

1. Spray a rimmed sheet pan with coconut oil. Preheat the oven to 325°.
2. Follow Steps 1–2 above, mixing the ingredients in a good-sized bowl.
3. Spread the granola onto the sheet pan.
4. Bake 10 minutes. Stir if it's not finished browning. Bake 5–7 minutes more, or until it's as brown as you want. If you like chunky granola, don't stir. Let cool, and then store in an airtight container.

English Porridge

Makes 2 servings   *Prep Time: 5 minutes*   *from Margaret H.*

- 1½ cups milk
- 1½ cups water
- scant ½ teaspoon salt

- ½ cup dry rolled oats
- ½ cup steel-cut oats

Stove Top
Cooking Time: 20 minutes

1. In a medium saucepan, stir together all ingredients.
2. Cook on medium heat, covered, until just simmering. Watch carefully so it doesn't boil over.
3. Turn heat to low. Stir often.
4. Cook 10–15 minutes, uncovered, until the mixture thickens and the steel-cut oats are chewy.
5. Serve with fruit or cream or whatever you like with cooked oatmeal.

OR a Microwave
Cooking Time: 10½ minutes

1. Mix all ingredients in a tall, narrow, microwave-safe, 3-quart container.
2. Cook uncovered on High 7½ minutes. Stir. (The advantage with the microwave is that you don't need to worry about the porridge sticking or boiling over—if you have a tall enough container. Try a 3-quart pyrex bowl.)
3. Cook uncovered on High 3 minutes.
4. Follow Step 5 above.

FRUITS & OTHER SWEETS

Berry Cobbler

4 - 5 servings   *Prep Time: 15 minutes*

- 1 cup flour
- ½ cup sugar
- 1 teaspoon baking powder
- ½ cup milk

- 2 cups fresh or frozen blueberries, raspberries, *or* blackberries, *or* some combination of them

Oven
Baking Time: 40 minutes

1. Grease a 9″ × 9″ baking dish. Preheat the oven to 350°.
2. Mix the dry ingredients together well. Then stir in the milk til smooth.
3. Spread into the baking dish.
4. Spoon the berries over top.
5. Bake 40 minutes, or til the berries are bubbling and a toothpick inserted into the center of the batter (which will rise to the top) comes out clean.
6. Serve warm with ice cream, yogurt, or milk if you want.

OR a 4- or 5-qt. Slow Cooker
Cooking Time: 2 - 2½ hours

1. Grease the crock.
2. Follow Steps 2 – 4 above, mixing the batter in the crock.
3. Cover, venting the lid with the handle of a wooden spoon laid across the crock. Cook on High 2 – 2½ hours, or until a toothpick inserted into the center of the cobbler comes out clean. Let stand 10 minutes, uncovered, before serving.
4. Follow Step 6 if you wish.

Minty Peach Cobbler

8 - 10 servings   **Prep Time: 30 minutes**

- 8 cups sliced fresh (peeled or not), *or* frozen, peaches
- 1 stick (8 tablespoons) butter softened to room temperature

- ¾ cup sugar
- 1 cup flour
- 10 fresh mint leaves, chopped, *or* 2 tablespoons dried chopped mint

4- or 5-qt. Slow Cooker
Cooking Time: 3 hours

1. Grease the interior of the crock. Spoon in the sliced peaches.
2. Cream the butter and sugar together. Stir in the flour til well mixed.
3. Crumble over the peaches.
4. Partially cover the crock by venting the lid. Lay the handle of a wooden spoon across the crock and under the lid.
5. Cook on High 3 hours, or until the peach juice bubbles around the edges, and a toothpick stuck into the center of the topping comes out clean.
6. Uncover the crock. Immediately sprinkle the cobbler with mint leaves.
7. Let cool til warm. Serve with milk or ice cream. Or as is.

OR an Oven
Baking Time: 60 - 70 minutes

1. Preheat the oven to 325°.
2. Place the prepared peaches in a greased 9″ × 13″ baking pan.
3. Follow Steps 2 & 3 above.
4. Bake 60 – 70 minutes, or until bubbly and a toothpick stuck into the center of the topping comes out clean.
5. Remove the pan from the oven. Scatter mint leaves over top.
6. Follow Step 7 above.

Crumbly Apple Crisp

8 servings   *Prep Time: 20 minutes*

- 6 – 8 large apples
- 1½ cups dry quick oats
- 1 – 1⅓ cups brown sugar, depending on how sweet the apples are
- ¾ cup flour
- 1½ sticks (12 tablespoons) butter, chilled and chunked

 Oven
Baking Time: 40 minutes

1. Grease a 9″ × 9″ baking dish. Preheat the oven to 350°.

2. Core and slice the apples, peeled or not. Place in the baking dish.

3. Stir the dry oats, brown sugar, and flour together in a bowl. Cut in the butter with a pastry cutter or 2 knives until crumbly. Spoon over the apples.

4. Bake 40 minutes, or til the apples are bubbly and the topping is golden. Let stand 10 minutes before serving.

5. Serve warm or cold with ice cream, milk, whipped cream, or yogurt.

Optional Ingredients and Variation:

- Or use pears, apricots, rhubarb, berries, or peaches. Or any combination of fruit that you like or have on hand.
- Add ¾ teaspoon ground cinnamon to Step 3.

 OR a 5- or 6-qt. slow cooker
Cooking Time: 3½ - 4 hours

1. Follow Steps 2 – 3 above, putting ingredients in the cooker.

2. Cover the cooker. Bake on High 3 – 3½ hours, or til the apples are bubbling and the batter has firmed up in the middle.

3. Uncover. Bake 30 more minutes to firm up the batter.

4. Let stand 20 minutes before serving. Follow Step 5 above.

Caramel Custard

8 servings   **Prep Time: 20 minutes**   **Standing/Cooling Time:
30 minutes – 2 hours**

- 1½ cups sugar, *divided*
- 6 eggs

- 2 teaspoons vanilla extract
- 3 cups milk

Stove Top and Oven
Cooking/Baking Time: 40 – 45 minutes

1. Grease eight 5- or 6-ounce ramekins. Preheat the oven to 350°.
2. Cook ¾ cup sugar in a heavy saucepan over low heat, stirring continually just until the sugar melts and turns golden.
3. Divide the caramel equally among the 8 ramekins. Tilt each one to coat the bottom of the cup. Let stand 10 minutes.
4. Meanwhile, mix together the remaining sugar, the eggs, vanilla, and milk til well combined but not foamy.
5. Spoon the mixture over the caramel in each cup, dividing it equally.
6. Set the cups into 2 8″ × 8″ baking dishes. Pour in boiling water 1 inch deep in each of the baking dishes.
7. Bake 40 – 45 minutes, or til a knife inserted into the center of the custards comes out clean.
8. Remove the ramekins from the baking dishes and let cool on wire racks.
9. When ready to serve, run a knife around the edge of each cup and invert the custard onto individual plates. Serve warm or cold.

OR a 6- or 7-qt. Slow Cooker
Cooking Time: 3 – 5 hours

1. Grease the interior of a round baking dish that will sit flat on the floor of the crock.
2. Place *all* the sugar into the dish. Cook on High, uncovered, 1 – 2 hours, tilting the dish now and then to coat the bottom.
3. Follow Steps 4 and 5 above, spooning the mixture over the caramel so it's not disturbed.
4. Cover the cooker. Cook on Low 2 – 3 more hours.
5. Place the baking dish on a wire rack to cool.
6. When it's fully cool, run a knife around the edge of the baking dish. Invert the custard onto a large plate. Slice and serve, spooning the caramel over top.

Orange-Flavored French-Toast Bread Pudding

Makes 6 - 8 servings   *Prep Time: 10 minutes*   *Standing Time: 30 minutes*

- 1½ cups orange juice
- 2½ cups milk
- 6 large eggs, beaten

- 12 slices sturdy bread, cubed or torn into ¾-inch pieces
- ½ to 1 cup maple syrup, warmed if you want

Oven
Baking Time: 1 hour

1. Preheat the oven to 350°. Grease a 9" × 13" baking dish.
2. Mix orange juice, milk, and eggs together well.
3. Put half the cubed bread into the baking dish. Pour half the liquid ingredients over top. Mix together well, stirring up from the bottom.
4. Put in the remaining bread. Pour the rest of the liquid mixture over top. Push the bread cubes down into the sauce without smashing the cubes.
5. Bake 1 hour, or til the bread is lightly browned. Let stand 30 minutes.
6. Top individual servings with drizzles of maple syrup.

OR a 6-qt. Slow Cooker
Cooking Time: 4 hours

1. Grease the interior of the crock.
2. Follow Steps 2 – 4 above, putting the ingredients into the crock.
3. Cover. Cook on Low 4 hours, or until the bread pudding is set.
4. Uncover and let the bread pudding stand for 30 minutes or so. Serve warm, topped with maple syrup.

Oatmeal Shortbread Bars

16 bars   **Prep Time: 15 minutes**   *from Joanna R-McD.*

- 1⅓ cups flour
- 2 sticks (16 tablespoons) butter, softened to room temperature

- ⅔ cup uncooked old-fashioned oatmeal
- ⅔ cup brown sugar
- ⅔ cup finely shredded coconut

Oven

Baking Time: 35 minutes

1. Preheat the oven to 300°.
2. Mix all ingredients together with your hands in a large bowl.
3. Pat into an ungreased 8-inch square baking pan.
4. Bake 35 minutes. For the best flavor, remove the shortbread from the oven when it's lightly browned, not dark.
5. Allow to cool completely before cutting into squares.

Optional ingredients:

- 8 glazed cherries, cut in half
- 16 pecan halves

These bars are a family favorite at Christmas-time. Before baking them, I imagine the cut lines for the 16 individual squares. Then I place either half a glazed cherry, cut side down, or half a pecan, on top of each square, before sticking them into the oven.

The bars are too rich to eat in large pieces, so I cut them fairly small. We love them with hot tea.

Peanut Butter Protein Balls

Makes 14 balls   **Prep Time: 5 minutes**   *from Kim L.*

- ⅔ cup organic peanut butter, smooth or chunky
- ½ cup organic mini-semi-sweet chocolate chips

- 1 cup uncooked old-fashioned oatmeal
- ½ cup ground flaxseed
- 2 tablespoons honey

 No Cooking

1. Combine all ingredients in a bowl.
2. Scoop out the dough with a ⅛ cup cookie scoop. Roll into balls.
3. Store in an airtight container for up to 1 week.

Tip:

If you'll be using natural peanut butter that you store in the fridge, set it out to soften for an hour before mixing the dough.

Almond Butter Cookies

16 servings

Prep Time: 10 minutes
Cooling Time: 10 minutes

from Kristina S.

- 1 cup almond butter, *or* nut butter of your choice, softened to room temperature
- 1 cup coconut sugar

- 1 large egg at room temperature
- 1 teaspoon baking soda
- 1 teaspoon pure vanilla extract

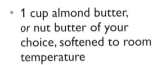

Oven
Baking Time: 9 - 10 minutes

1. Preheat the oven to 350°. Move the 2 oven racks close to the center of the oven.

2. Place all ingredients in a large bowl and stir to combine.

3. For best results, cover your baking sheet with parchment or a silicone mat. Scoop out the dough in medium-sized balls (about 1½ tablespoons each) onto the baking sheet. Place the balls about 2 inches apart because they'll spread.

4. Use a fork to press a crisscross pattern on the top of each cookie.

5. Bake 9 - 10 minutes, until the edges are set and the centers are puffed.

6. Cool for about 10 minutes before enjoying!

Variations:

1. You can substitute white or brown sugar for the coconut sugar.

2. Add ½ cup of chocolate chips in Step 2 for chocolate-lovers.

Tips:

1. The cookies will keep in an airtight container for 1 week.

2. This is a tasty and easy dessert to make for friends and family who follow a gluten-free diet.

Juicy Cooked Apples

6 - 8 servings   **Prep Time: 10 - 15 minutes**

- 8 cups organic apple slices, peeled or not
- no sugar, or maybe $1/3 - 1/2$ cup, depending on the sweetness of the apples

- water
- $1\frac{1}{2} - 2$ cups raisins

Stove Top
Cooking Time: 15 - 20 minutes

1. Core and cut the apples into quarters or eighths, depending on their size and your preference. Pour into a saucepan.

2. If the apples are sweet, skip the sugar. Or add just enough to enhance the flavor of the fruit.

3. Add an inch or two of water (between your pointer finger's first and second knuckles) and stir together.

4. Stir in as many raisins as you want.

5. Cook *slowly* over medium low heat, stirring up frequently. Stop cooking the moment the rawness is broken down. You want defined slices, not applesauce.

6. Eat warm or cold, as a side dish to a main meal, or as a cereal or cake or ice cream topping.

OR a 4- or 5-qt. Slow Cooker
Cooking Time: 2 - 3 hours

1. Put all the ingredients into the crock.

2. Cover. Cook on Low $2-3$ hours, or just until the rawness of the apples is gone.

3. See Step 6 above.

Strawberry Frozen Yogurt Popsicles

6 servings   ***Prep Time: 10 minutes.***   *from Kim L.*

- 2 tablespoons honey
- ½ cup plain Greek yogurt, non-fat *or* full-fat

- 2 cups frozen strawberries
- ½ tablespoon fresh lemon juice

 No Cooking
Freezing Time: 6 - 8 hours

1. Put honey and yogurt in a food processor and mix until fully combined.

2. Add in frozen strawberries and lemon juice. Process 2 – 3 minutes, or until creamy. Scrape down the sides and process again until there are no lumps left.

3. Pour into popsicle molds and freeze until solid, 6 – 8 hours, or overnight.

Variations:

Replace the strawberries and lemon juice to make the following variations:

- Mango Lime: 2 cups frozen mango, plus the juice and zest from one lime

- Strawberry Banana: 1 cup frozen strawberries, 1 cup frozen bananas, ½ tablespoon fresh lemon juice

- Mango Strawberry: 1 cup frozen strawberries, 1 cup frozen mango, ½ tablespoon fresh lemon juice

- Raspberry Peach: 1 cup frozen peaches, 1 cup frozen raspberries, 1 tablespoon fresh lemon juice

- Pineapple Coconut: 2 cups frozen pineapple, ½ tablespoon fresh lemon juice, 2 tablespoons toasted coconut

To make Scoopable Frozen Yogurt:

After combining all of the ingredients in a food processor, pour the mixture into a small freezer-safe container. Place in the freezer, stirring every hour to keep it from getting too solid. Serve when it reaches the consistency of ice cream.

Butter Roasted Plantains (or Bananas) with Orange Sauce

6 servings   **Prep Time: 10 minutes**

- 3 quite ripe plantains, *or* bananas
- ¼ stick (2 tablespoons) butter

- ¾ cup orange juice
- 1 teaspoon grated orange rind
- ¼ teaspoon ground cinnamon

Oven
Baking Time: 20 - 25 minutes

1. Grease a 7″ × 9″ baking dish. Preheat the oven to 375°.
2. Peel the plantains or bananas and cut them in half length-wise. Or cut them in coins about ½″ thick. Place in baking dish.
3. Drop small chunks of butter over the slices. Pour the oj over top.
4. Scatter with the orange rind and cinnamon.
5. Bake uncovered 20 – 25 minutes, basting with the oj from time to time.
6. If you wish, serve with whipped cream, plain or vanilla yogurt, or ice cream.

Optional Ingredients:

If you wish, pour 2 – 3 tablespoons light rum over the bananas in Step 3. And sprinkle some brown sugar over the dish in Step 4.

OR a Stove Top
Cooking Time: 10 minutes

1. Melt the butter in a large skillet.
2. Stir in the oj, orange rind, and cinnamon. Stir frequently over low heat til the mixture becomes syrupy and bubbly.
3. Remove the skillet from the heat and plunge in the sliced plaintains or bananas. Cook 5 – 7 minutes, or until the fruit is softened and infused with the sauce flavors.
4. Follow Step 6 above.

Applesauce Heaven

8 - 10 servings   *Prep Time: 20 minutes*   *from Barbara L.*

- 12 or more organic apples (enough to fill your slow cooker), cored, NOT peeled, cut into chunks

- 1 tablespoon ground cinnamon
- 1½ cups unsweetened apple cider

 5- or 6-qt. Slow Cooker
Cooking Time: 4 - 5 hours

1. Place the apples chunks in a 5- or 6-quart slow cooker. (Apple sizes vary, so just fill your slow cooker, allowing enough room to stir in the other ingredients.)
2. Stir in cinnamon and apple cider.
3. Cover. Cook 4–5 hours on Low, or until the apples are soft.
4. Use an immersion blender to make the sauce as smooth as you like.
5. Chill. Serve with a meal or as dessert. It's also a great dessert topping.

OR a 6-qt. Electric Pressure Cooker
Cooking Time: 6 minutes; 25 minutes to natural-release the pressure

1. Stir all the ingredients together in the cooker.
2. Pressure cook on High 6 minutes (valve closed; Keep Warm setting off).
3. Natural-release the pressure; about 25 minutes.
4. Follow Steps 4 and 5 above.

Tips:

1. Chunky sauce is incredible on pancakes. I have a friend who eats the chunky sauce on his ice cream. This recipe also has fans who love it in its chunky state on breakfast oatmeal.
2. The smooth version can substitute for butter in some recipes.
3. I vary and mix the types of apples I use and vary the size of the slow cooker according to the amount of apples. However, I always use organics so I don't have to peel.

APPETIZERS, SNACKS, & BEVERAGES

Refried Beans and Cheese Dip

4 - 5 cups   ***Prep Time: 5 minutes***

- 16-ounce can organic refried beans
- 1 cup sour cream

- 1 cup Salsa-In-No-Time (recipe on page 176)
- 1 cup shredded mozzarella *or* cheddar cheese

 Oven
Baking Time: 15 minutes

1. Grease a pie plate or shallow baking dish. Preheat the oven to 350°.

2. Put a layer of beans in the dish. Follow that with layers of the next 3 ingredients in order.

3. Bake for about 15 minutes, or til the cheese melts and the Dip is hot through.

4. Serve with fresh, cut-up vegs and/or taco chips or favorite crackers.

 OR a Microwave
Cooking Time: 2 minutes

1. Follow Steps 1 and 2 above, using a microwave-safe dish.

2. Heat on Power 8 for 1½ – 2 minutes, or til the cheese has melted and the Dip is hot through. If the Dip needs more time, mic it in 15-second intervals on Power 8.

3. Follow Step 4.

Fruity Salsa

2½ - 3 cups   **Prep Time: 15 - 20 minutes**   **Chilling Time: 4 - 24 hour**

- 2 cups or so of a combination of chopped fresh fruit—apples, pears, peaches, apricots, pineapples, kiwi, mangoes, papaya, strawberries

- 1 good-sized sweet onion, red or yellow, chopped

- ⅓ – ½ cup of your favorite chili peppers, cores and seeds removed, and the peppers chopped

 No Cooking

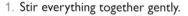

1. Stir everything together gently.

2. Cover and refrigerate 4 – 24 hours so the flavors can combine.

3. Spread over grilled meat or use as a dip.

Salsa-In-No-Time

2½ - 3 cups   ***Prep Time: 10 - 15 minutes, depending on how much cutting and stripping of leaves you do***

- 2½ cups cut-up tomatoes
- half an onion, chunked
- ½–1 jalapeño, depending on how much heat you like, core and seeds removed

- 1¼ cups cilantro leaves (if a few stems are mixed in that won't hurt)
- ½–1 teaspoon salt, to taste

 No Cooking

1. Put everything into a food processor. Pulse for 10 seconds.
2. If you want a saucier salsa, process in 5-second increments til it's the consistency you want.

Optional Ingredients for Step 1:

- a garlic clove or two
- 2 teaspoons vinegar (you choose the kind)
- 2 teaspoons lemon juice
- 1 teaspoon olive oil

Black Bean Salsa

about 3½ cups   *Prep Time: 15 minutes*   *Chilling Time: 8 - 24 hours*

- 2 15-ounce cans organic black beans, drained and rinsed, *or* 4 cups of your own cooked beans

- 1 cup organic corn, fresh *or* canned (drained if canned)

- 1 large fresh tomato, chopped

- ⅓ – ½ cup fresh cilantro, chopped

- 4 tablespoons fresh lime juice

 No Cooking

1. Toss everything together gently in a good-sized bowl.

2. Cover. Refrigerate 8 – 24 hours so the flavors can combine.

3. Taste and adjust seasonings if needed.

4. Serve as a dip.

Optional Ingredients:

- Add salt and pepper to taste.

- Add minced garlic cloves, sliced scallions, and/or spring onions.

Pitch-Perfect Guacamole

5 cups   *Prep Time: 15 - 20 minutes*   *Chilling Time: 8 - 24 hours*

- 3 avocados
- ⅓ cup minced onion
- ½ teaspoon chili powder

- 2 tablespoons lemon juice
- 1 large ripe tomato, chopped

 No Cooking

1. Cut the avocados in half, remove the seeds, and scoop the good green stuff into a bowl.

2. Add the minced onion, chili powder, and lemon juice.

3. Use a masher to blend everything together til creamy and well mixed.

4. Fold in the chopped tomatoes.

5. Serve over toast or as a dip.

Optional Ingredient:

- For a little more zest, add ¾ teaspoon garlic powder in Step 2.

Hummus from Dried Chickpeas

3 - 4 cups   *Soaking Time: 8 - 24 hours, or overnight*   *Prep Time: 10 minutes*

- 1 pound dried chickpeas (garbanzo beans)
- ⅔ cup fresh lemon juice
- 3 cloves garlic, chopped
- ⅔ cup organic all-natural peanut butter, or Tahini (see MIY recipe on page 196)
- ½ cup chopped cilantro

Stove Top
Cooking Time: 1 - 1½ hours, or til chickpeas are tender

1. Put the dried chickpeas in a good-sized stockpot. Cover with water. Soak 8 hours, or overnight.

2. Drain off the soaking water and discard.

3. Cover with fresh water. Cover and cook over low to medium heat til the chickpeas are tender, 1 − 1½ hours.

4. Drain off the cooking liquid, but save some of it if you want to thin the finished hummus. Pour the cooked chickpeas into a food processor.

5. Add all other ingredients and process til smooth.

6. Taste and adjust seasoning and consistency. Cool to room temp.

7. Serve as a dip or sandwich filling.

Or a 5- or 6-qt. Slow Cooker
Cooking Time: 2 - 8 hours to cook soft, depending on the age of the beans; 4 hours to cool to room temp

1. Place soaked beans in the crock (should be about half-full).

2. Fill the crock with water.

3. Check the beans after they've cooked 2 hours. If they're nearly soft, they'll probably be done in another hour. If they're still pretty solid, cook them another 2 − 3 hours before checking again.

4. Let the beans come to room temperature in the cooking liquid to decrease their splitting open, about 4 hours.

5. Follow Steps 4 − 7 above.

Hummus from Canned Chickpeas

about 2 cups   *Prep Time: 10 minutes*

- 1 garlic clove, crushed
- 15-ounce can organic chickpeas, drained and rinsed
- 2 tablespoons fresh lemon juice

- ⅛ teaspoon dried cumin
- ⅓ cup organic tahini paste *or* MIY recipe on page 196
- 2 tablespoons water, if needed

 No Cooking

---

1. Pour all ingredients except the water into a food processor or blender.

2. Blend til smooth. Add water if you want a looser consistency.

3. Taste and adjust seasonings.

4. Pour into a serving dish or make sandwiches.

Roasted Pepper Spread

8 servings   **Prep Time: 10 minutes**   *from Kim M.*
                        Chilling Time: 1 - 48 hours

- 1 cup broken walnuts, ideally toasted
- 1½ cups of your own roasted peppers, *or* 12-oz. jar roasted peppers (nothing else added) well-drained

- 3 tablespoons lemon juice
- 1½ tablespoons unsulphured molasses
- ¾ teaspoon salt

 No Cooking

1. Process all ingredients in a food processor until smooth.

2. To allow the flavors to blend, cover and chill one hour or up to two days.

3. Serve with pita bread or crackers. Or serve with hummus, olives, cucumber chunks, and feta cheese for a Mediterranean-inspired appetizer tray.

Optional ingredients:

- ⅓ cup dry bread crumbs, *or* crushed crackers, to keep the liquid from separating
- 2 tablespoons olive oil

- ¼ teaspoon cayenne for a spicier spread
- 2 tablespoons pomegranate molasses for a richer flavor

Spicy Cranberry Dip

about 2 cups

Prep Time: 5 minutes
(if the Cranberry Sauce from Scratch is ready to go)

- 1 batch Cranberry Sauce from Scratch (recipe on page 63)
- 1 tablespoon organic prepared mustard

- 3 tablespoons organic prepared horseradish
- wheel of camembert cheese (about 5 inches across) *and/ or* half a wheel of brie (about 9–17 inches across)

Stove Top
Cooking Time: 10 minutes

1. Heat cranberry sauce, mustard, and horseradish together just til warmed, about 10 minutes.

2. Spoon half the dip over a wheel of camembert and the remainder over half a wheel of brie.

3. Set out crackers and knives and watch the dip, cheese, and crackers disappear.

OR a Microwave
Cooking Time: 1 - 1½ minutes

1. Stir the cranberry sauce, mustard, and horseradish together in a microwave-safe bowl.

2. Mic on High 1–1½ minutes, or til warmed through but not boiling.

3. Continue with Steps 2 and 3 above.

Nepali Spiced Tea

6 servings **Prep Time: 5 minutes**

- 3 tablespoons black tea leaves, *or* 3 tea bags black tea
- 5 cups boiling water
- 1 1/4 cups milk

- 1/3 – 2/3 cup sugar
- 4 whole cloves
- 2 – 3 cardamom pods, cracked open, *or* 1/2 teaspoon ground cardamom

Stove Top
Cooking Time: 20 minutes

1. Heat water to boiling in a good-sized saucepan. Steep the tea leaves in a tea ball 5 minutes.

2. Heat the milk to scalding in a separate pan. When the tea is steeped, stir in the milk, sugar, cloves, and cardamom.

3. Simmer 10 minutes for good flavor, stirring now and then to make sure the sugar is dissolved.

4. Remove the tea leaves and serve hot.

Optional Ingredients:

Add 1 cinnamon stick to Step 2. Remove before serving.

OR a Microwave
Cooking Time: 7 1/2 minutes

1. Heat the water in a microwave-safe container on High for 3 minutes, or until it boils. Begin steeping the tea; continue for 5 minutes.

2. Heat the milk in a separate microwave-safe container on High for 1 1/2 minutes, or til it is scalding.

3. Stir the tea, milk, sugar, cloves, and cardamom together and mic on High for 3 minutes.

4. Continue with Step 4 above.

Rich Ginger Tea

8 servings   **Prep Time: 7 minutes**

- 4 cups water
- 2 tablespoons diced ginger root
- 3½ tablespoons sugar

- 4 cups milk of your choice
- 3½ tablespoons black tea leaves in a tea ball, *or* 10 tea bags of black tea

4-qt. Slow Cooker
Cooking Time: 3½ hours

1. Mix water, ginger root, and sugar in the crock of a 4-quart slow cooker.
2. Cover. Cook on High 2 hours.
3. Stir in milk.
4. Cover. Cook on High 30 minutes, or until completely hot. Do not boil.
5. Turn off the cooker. Stir in the tea. Cover and let steep 20 minutes.
6. Strain out the diced ginger and any tea leaves that escaped.
7. Serve hot.

Tip:

Turn the cooker to warm during Step 7 if you want to keep the tea warm for an extended period of time. It will stay hot without fear that it will cook dry.

OR a Stove Top
Cooking Time: 10 - 15 minutes to heat; 20 minutes to steep

1. Bring the water, ginger root, and sugar to a boil over high heat in a covered 4-quart saucepan.
2. Stir in the milk. Heat 5–7 minutes over medium heat, just til it's scalding hot but not boiling.
3. Continue with Steps 5–7 above.

The fresh ginger gives this tea a bit of sting!

Crab-Stuffed Mushrooms

8 - 12 servings　　　**Prep Time: 30 minutes**

- 12 big white, *or* cremini, mushrooms, 2 – 2½ inches across

- 2 slices of bread, toasted

- 6 ounces crabmeat, shell and cartilage removed

- 1 egg

- 1 cup grated cheddar *or* fontina cheese

Oven
Baking Time: 30 minutes

1. Cut the stems off the mushroom tops.

2. Chop the stems and toasted bread together in a food processor, or by hand. Place in a mixing bowl.

3. Fold in the crabmeat and egg.

4. Grease a 9" × 13" baking dish. Preheat the oven to 375°.

5. Stuff the mushroom tops with the mixture. Place the filled tops in the baking dish in a single layer, stuffed-side up.

6. Bake 20 minutes.

7. Scatter grated cheese over top. Bake 10 more minutes, or til the cheese is melted and browned.

MIY
SAUCES

189

Italian Soffritto

3½ cups   **Prep Time: 20 minutes**   *from Kristin O.*

- 2 medium to large yellow or white onions
- 2 celery ribs

- 2 large carrots
- 2 fat garlic cloves
- 2 tablespoons olive oil

Stove Top
Cooking Time: 10 - 12 minutes, or up to 45 minutes

1. Chop onions into ½-inch dice.
2. Chop celery into ¼-inch dice.
3. Chop carrots into ¼-inch dice.
4. Press the garlic cloves.
5. Sauté all vegs in oil til softened. To deepen the Soffritto's flavor, continue cooking over low heat for up to 45 minutes.
6. Refrigerate or freeze til needed.

OR a Microwave
Cooking Time: 3 - 5 minutes

1. Put the chopped onions, celery, carrots, garlic, and olive oil in a microwave-safe dish. Cover. Mic on High 3 minutes.
2. Stir and test how soft the vegs are. If you want them softer, cover and mic another 1 - 2 minutes.

MIY Onion-Garlic Base

1½ - 2 cups   ***Prep Time: 10 minutes***   *from Kim M.*

- 4 tablespoons vegetable *or* olive oil
- 3 large onions, minced

- 8 cloves garlic, minced
- ¼ teaspoon salt

Stove Top
Cooking Time: 10 minutes

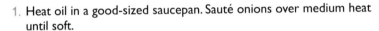

1. Heat oil in a good-sized saucepan. Sauté onions over medium heat until soft.
2. Add garlic and salt. Sauté 30 seconds, or until fragrant.
3. Remove from heat and cool.

Variations:

1. To tilt the Base in a gingery direction, add 2–4 tablespoons grated fresh ginger (depending on how much you like fresh ginger) in Step 2.

2. For more heat, add 2 tablespoons minced hot peppers in Step 2.

OR a 3- or 6-qt. Electric Pressure Cooker
Cooking Time: 5 minutes; 20 minutes to pressure-release naturally

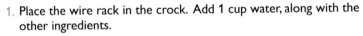

1. Place the wire rack in the crock. Add 1 cup water, along with the other ingredients.
2. Pressure cook on High 5 minutes (valve closed; Keep Warm setting off).
3. Release pressure release naturally, about 20 minutes.

Roasted Tomato Sauce

4 - 5 servings   *Prep Time: 30 minutes*   *from Barbara L.*

- 2½ pounds tomatoes, quartered and cored, but not peeled
- 1 onion, diced

- 1 green and 1 red bell pepper, cut in 1" pieces
- ½ cup olive oil
- 1½ teaspoons salt

 5-qt. Slow Cooker
Cooking Time: 5 hours

1. Toss together the tomatoes, onions, peppers, oil, and salt in the cooker.

2. Cover and cook on Low 5 hours.

3. Use your immersion blender to make the sauce as smooth or as chunky as you like.

Optional ingredients to add in Step 1: ¼ teaspoon red pepper flakes, ¼ cup chopped fresh basil, 2 teaspoons fresh oregano, minced garlic to taste

 OR an Oven
Roasting Time: 40 minutes

1. Preheat the oven to 400°. Pour half the olive oil onto a sheet pan. Top with half the diced onions and chopped peppers.

2. Core the tomatoes and halve them. Lay them over top, cut side down.

3. Spoon the remaining onions and peppers over all, and then the olive oil.

4. Roast 30 minutes. Scatter any optional ingredients over top that you want.

5. Either way, roast 10 more minutes. Pinch off the skins with your fingers.

6. Mash with a potato masher. Taste and add seasonings if needed.

Tip:

1. If you have a garden or a market nearby where you can easily get tomatoes, you can double the recipe. You may need to add an extra hour of cooking time for the larger quantity. Use what you want to eat now, and freeze the extra to use later.

2. Eat this as tomato soup if you blend it til it's smoother. Or leave it chunky and serve it as a pasta sauce.

Adobo Sauce

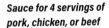

Sauce for 4 servings of pork, chicken, or beef   ***Prep Time: 10 minutes***   ***Standing Time: 30 minutes***

- ¼ cup organic apple cider vinegar
- ¼ cup organic soy sauce
- 3 garlic cloves, minced

- 2 tablespoons sugar
- 3–4 crushed peppercorns, *or* ¼ teaspoon black pepper
- ½–¾ cup water

 No Cooking

1. Combine everything well.
2. Let stand 30 minutes so flavors can blend.
3. Keep in the fridge til needed for Pork, Chicken, or Beef Adobo.

Optional ingredient:

- Add 1 bay leaf in Step 1.

Tahini Sauce

2¾ cups   ***Prep Time: 10 - 15 minutes***

- 1½ cups organic tahini (sesame seed) paste
- 1 cup water
- ½ cup fresh lemon juice

- 3 – 4 garlic cloves, minced
- ½ teaspoon smoked paprika
- ¼ teaspoon coarsely ground black pepper

No Cooking

1. Purée the tahini and water in a blender. Or beat with a wooden spoon til well mixed.
2. Add all the remaining ingredients and blend, or beat, til creamy.
3. Use as a dip, a salad dressing, and a topping for savory bowls.

Optional ingredient:

- Add a tablespoon of chopped fresh parsley and/or part of a minced hot pepper.

Yogurt Sauce, or Raita

1 cup **Prep Time: 3 minutes** **Standing Time: 30 minutes**

- 1 cup plain yogurt (full-fat works best)
- 1 teaspoon ground coriander
- ½ teaspoon ground cumin
- ½ teaspoon ground turmeric

 No Cooking

1. Mix all ingredients together.

2. Let stand at least 30 minutes so flavors can blend.

3. Use as a dip with naan or falafel. Use it on curries and kebabs, from seafood to lamb.

Optional ingredients:

- Grate a cucumber. Mix in ¼ teaspoon salt. Let stand 30 minutes. Then squeeze out as much of the water as you can. Fold the grated cucumber into the sauce.

- Pound a packed cup of fresh mint leaves into a mortar with a tablespoon of water. Use a pestle to crush it. Fold it into the sauce.

Tzatziki Sauce

1½ cups servings   ***Prep Time: 30 minutes***   *from Margaret H.*

- 1 medium cucumber, peeled or not
- ½ teaspoon salt and ¼ teaspoon freshly ground pepper

- 2 garlic cloves
- 2 tablespoons chopped fresh mint *or* dill
- 1 cup plain yogurt

 No Cooking

1. Grate the cucumber. Sprinkle with salt and place on a kitchen towel.
2. Allow to sit 10–20 minutes.
3. Wrap the grated cucumber in the towel and squeeze out the liquid over the sink.
4. Chop the garlic cloves and then mash with the side of the knife.
5. Combine the cucumber, garlic, and the rest of the ingredients.

Optional ingredient:

- zest of half a lemon *or* lime

Tips:

1. De-seed the cucumber first if the cucumber is large and the seeds are big.
2. Serve over falafel or with tomatoes as a summer sandwich.
3. Stir into greens for a cooling salad with any Middle Eastern dish.

Sriracha Mayo

⅓ cup   **Prep Time: 5 minutes**   *from Kim L.*

- ¼ cup plain Greek yogurt
- 2 tablespoons sriracha sauce, ideally homemade
- 1 teaspoon chili powder

No Cooking

1. Fold all ingredients together until well mixed.
2. Store any leftovers in a container with a tight-fitting lid.

Tip:

1. Serve on Black Bean Burgers (recipe on page 46) and Sweet Potato Fries with Caramelized Kimchi (recipe on page 131). And anything else that tempts you!
2. Make it ahead and store in the refrigerator for up to 2 months.

Variation:

Or use store-bought sriracha with your favorite mix of hot peppers, checking that there are no stabilizers or extenders in the sauce.

MIY Cheddar Sauce (and Creamy Mushroom Sauce)

1½ cups   *Prep Time: 10 minutes*   *from Meredith M.*

- 3 tablespoons butter
- 2 tablespoons minced onion
- 3 tablespoons flour

- 1 cup whole milk
- 2 cups of your favorite cheddar cheese, shredded

 Stove Top
Cooking Time: 10 minutes

1. In a small saucepan, sauté the onions in butter until tender.
2. Add flour and stir until smooth. Cook at least 1 minute.
3. Gradually add milk to the saucepan, whisking the whole time.
4. Stirring frequently, cook until the sauce bubbles and thickens.
5. Take off the heat and add the cheddar cheese. Stir until melted and totally incorporated.

Variation:

I often add some finely chopped mushrooms to the first step and omit the cheddar in the final step to make a Creamy Mushroom Sauce.

 OR a Microwave (which is very quick and easy!)
Cooking Time: 2½ - 3½ minutes

1. Place butter and minced onions together in a microwave-safe bowl. Mic on High 1 minute.
2. Whisk in flour. Mic on High 30 seconds.
3. Whisk in milk. Mic on High 30 seconds. Whisk to smooth out any lumps. Continue mic-ing in 30-second intervals, whisking after each time, until thickened and smooth.
4. Pick up with Step 5 above.

Pine Nut Sauce

½ - ¾ cup   **Prep Time: 10 minutes**   *from Kim L.*

- ½ cup raw pine nuts *
- 5 tablespoons extra-virgin olive oil
- 1 tablespoon fresh lemon juice

Stove Top
Cooking Time: 5 - 7 minutes

1. In a skillet over medium heat, toast the pine nuts until golden.

2. Transfer to a mini food processor along with the oil and lemon juice. Blend until smooth. Set aside until the pasta is cooked.

* While you can substitute other nuts, pine nuts are really worth it when you're adding it to cooked pasta and a sauce of fresh tomatoes and herbs.

MIY
SEASONING
MIXES

MIY Chili Seasoning

rounded ½ cup | **Prep Time: 5 minutes** | *from Kristina S.*

- ¼ cup chili powder
- 1 tablespoon paprika
- 1 tablespoon cumin

- 1 teaspoon garlic powder
- 4 teaspoons sea salt and 2 teaspoons ground black pepper

No Cooking

1. Place spices in a small bowl and whisk to combine.

2. Place in an airtight container and store in a cool dry place.

3. Use ¼ cup of this seasoning per pot of chili (see recipe for No-Beans Chili on page 24) that serves 8–10 people.

Optional ingredient:

- For more heat, add 1 teaspoon cayenne pepper.

Middle East Spice Blend

1 rounded tablespoon   **Prep Time: 2 minutes**   *from Margaret H.*

- 1 teaspoon ground cinnamon
- 1 teaspoon salt
- ½ teaspoon ground nutmeg

- ½ teaspoon ground allspice
- ½ teaspoon black pepper

 No Cooking

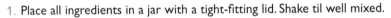

1. Place all ingredients in a jar with a tight-fitting lid. Shake til well mixed.
2. Use immediately, or store in a cool dark place for up to 6 months.

Saag Seasoning Mix

1 tablespoon + 1 teaspoon   **Prep Time: 1 - 2 minutes**   *from Laura K.*

- 2 teaspoons ground coriander
- ½ teaspoon turmeric

- 1½ teaspoons salt

No Cooking

1. Shake all together in a small jar with a tight-fitting lid.
2. Store in a cool dark place til needed, up to 6 months.

Dal Seasoning Mix

2 tablespoons   *Prep Time: 2 - 5 minutes*   *from Laura K.*

- ½ teaspoon turmeric
- ¼ teaspoon chili powder
- 1 teaspoon cumin

- 1½ teaspoons salt
- 1 tablespoon Garam Masala (see recipe on page 212)

 No Cooking

1. Shake all together in a small jar with a tight-fitting lid.
2. Store in a cool dark place til needed, up to 6 months.

Seasoned Bread Crumbs

2 cups **Prep Time: 5 - 7 minutes**

- 4 slices stale bread, cubed
- 1 teaspoon dried oregano
- ¼ teaspoon dried thyme
- ¼ teaspoon smoked paprika

Oven
Baking Time: 8 - 12 minutes

1. Preheat the oven to 350°.
2. Drop all the ingredients into a blender or food processor. Grind into crumbs, as fine or as coarse as you like.
3. Spread mixture onto a rimmed sheet pan.
4. Bake 8 – 12 minutes, stirring now and then so the crumbs brown all over but don't burn.
5. Let cool. Store in an airtight container.

Garam Masala Seasoning Mix

3 tablespoons   **Prep Time: 3 minutes**   *from Laura K.*

- 1 tablespoon ground coriander
- 2 teaspoons coarsely ground black pepper

- 2 teaspoons ground cardamom
- 1 teaspoon ground cinnamon
- 1 teaspoon ground cloves

 No Cooking

1. Mix together until fully combined.
2. Store what's left in an airtight container for future meals.

Italian Herb Mix

¼ - ⅓ cup   **Prep Time: 5 - 7 minutes**

- 3 tablespoons dried basil
- 1 tablespoon dried oregano
- 1 tablespoon dried parsley flakes

- ¾ teaspoon chopped dried rosemary leaves
- dash of cayenne pepper

 No Cooking

1. Mix everything together in a small bowl.
2. Use as a rub for meat, or include in a marinade for meat or vegetables.
3. Store in an airtight container.

Seasoned Croutons

1 quart **Prep Time: 20 minutes** *from Meredith M.*

- 1 loaf of sturdy bread, partially frozen (to make cutting easier)
- 2½ sticks (20 tablespoons) butter, melted
- 1 teaspoon black pepper
- 2 teaspoons organic garlic salt
- ¾ cup grated Parmesan cheese

 Oven

Baking Time: Approximately 1 hour

1. Preheat the oven to 250°.
2. While the bread is still partially frozen, cut it into ¾-inch cubes. Place in a large bowl.
3. In a small bowl, mix the melted butter with the remaining ingredients.
4. Drizzle over the bread cubes. Toss till evenly coated.
5. Place on a lightly greased rimmed baking sheet. Dry in the oven until crisp, about an hour.

Tips:

1. I like to play around with different seasonings that will go well with whatever I'm serving.
2. Sprinkle the croutons on salads and soups and on top of baked savory dishes.

Black Bean Soup Seasoning Mix

3⅓ tablespoons   **Prep Time: 2 minutes**   *from Laura K.*

- 2 teaspoons salt
- 2 teaspoons cumin

- 2 tablespoons lemon juice

No Cooking

1. Shake all together in a small jar with a tight-fitting lid.
2. Refrigerate til needed, up to **1** month.

Herb Butter—to make anything savory taste better!

½ cup   ***Prep Time: 5 minutes***

- 1 stick (8 tablespoons) unsalted butter, softened
- 2 tablespoons chopped fresh basil
- 2 tablespoons chopped fresh chives
- 1 teaspoon lemon juice
- salt and pepper to taste

 No Cooking

1. Beat butter til light and airy.
2. Fold in all remaining ingredients.
3. Cover. Chill until you're ready to use it—on cooked vegetables, in soups, on cooked meats (as a chilled square or daub), on breads…

Variation:

Change up the fresh herbs to whatever is growing in your pot or patch, or whatever you most enjoy.

Index

About the Author

Phyllis Good is a *New York Times* bestselling author whose cookbooks have sold more than 14,000,000 copies.

Her cookbooks are beloved for their outstandingly flavorful recipes which are easy to follow and quick to prepare. Phyllis is the originator of the phenomenal "Fix-It and Forget-It" series and, most recently, author of **Stock the Crock** cookbook.

She loves to empower those who are short on time and short on confidence in the kitchen, so they can "prepare delicious food for those who gather around their tables."

For more information about this book and other titles published by Walnut Street Books, please visit **www.walnutstreetbooks.com**.

To receive brief monthly updates about upcoming books and other news, sign up at **www.walnutstreetbooks.com/#updates**

For bulk orders of this book, contact: info@walnutstreetbooks.com